The Quest for Human Dignity
in the
Ethics of Pregnancy Termination

The Quest for Human Dignity
in the
Ethics of Pregnancy Termination

Tom J. Obengo

WIPF & STOCK · Eugene, Oregon

THE QUEST FOR HUMAN DIGNITY IN THE ETHICS OF PREGNANCY TERMINATION

Copyright © 2016 Tom J. Obengo. All rights reserved. Except for brief quotations in critical publications or reviews, no part of this book may be reproduced in any manner without prior written permission from the publisher. Write: Permissions, Wipf and Stock Publishers, 199 W. 8th Ave., Suite 3, Eugene, OR 97401.

Wipf & Stock
An Imprint of Wipf and Stock Publishers
199 W. 8th Ave., Suite 3
Eugene, OR 97401

www.wipfandstock.com

PAPERBACK ISBN: 978-1-4982-3382-8
HARDCOVER ISBN: 978-1-4982-3384-2
EBOOK ISBN: 978-1-4982-3383-5

Manufactured in the U.S.A. 06/15/2016

DECLARATION

I HEREBY DECLARE THAT the entirety of the work contained therein is my own, original work, that I am the sole author thereof, save to the extent explicitly otherwise stated, and that it was originally prepared as a thesis submitted in December 2013 in fulfilment of the requirements for the degree of Master of Theology in Systematic Theology, specialising in Medical Ethics, under the supervision of Dr. Chris Jones in the Department of Systematic Theology and Ecclesiology at the Faculty of Theology, University of Stellenbosch.

CONTENTS

Acknowledgments | ix
Preface | xi
Opsomming | xiii
Abbreviations | xv

CHAPTER 1
The Significant Challenge of Pregnancy Termination | 1

CHAPTER 2
Historical, Biblical and Theological-Ethical Perspectives on Termination of Pregnancy | 22

CHAPTER 3
Causes, Procedures and Consequences of Termination of Pregnancy | 53

CHAPTER 4
Theoretical and Conceptual Framework | 70

CHAPTER 5
Research Design and Methodology | 82

CHAPTER 6
Research Findings | 89

CHAPTER 7
Discussions, Evaluation and Recommendations | 110

CHAPTER 8
Conclusion | 129

APPENDIX 1: Structured Interviews and Focus Group Discussions | 133
APPENDIX 2: Glossary | 135

Bibliography | 141
Index | 149

ACKNOWLEDGMENTS

My foremost gratitude is to the Lord God Almighty who has given me life, sustained me, and brought me to this present time. In addition, I wish to express my deepest gratitude to:

- My supervisor, Dr. Chris Jones, of the Faculty of Theology at the University of Stellenbosch, whose supervision, guidance, support, advice and encouragement directly contributed to the successful completion of this study.
- The National Council for Science and Technology, Ministry of Higher Education in the Republic of Kenya, who granted me an official research permit through which I was able to carry out structured interviews and focused group discussions with various individuals and groups for this research.
- The Research Ethics Review Committee of Great Lakes University of Kisumu who granted me student affiliation status and carried out an ethical review of my research.
- The Faculty Board of the Faculty of Theology and the Research Ethics Committee (REC) at the University of Stellenbosch for giving the necessary clearance for the research.
- The academic, administrative and library staff of the Faculty of Theology at Stellenbosch for providing academic, administrative and logistical support during the entire period of my studies. Notable are Prof. Nico Koopman (Dean of Faculty), Prof. Robert Vosloo (Head of Department), and Mrs. Wilma Riekert (Faculty Administrative Officer).

Acknowledgments

- My wife, Dorothy, and my two daughters, Rebekka Mich and Hannah Gweth, for their unwavering support, constant encouragement and joyful willingness to allow time for me to study and write.
- My mother, Paskalia Awino Oria, for teaching me human virtues that formed the basis of my interest in the discipline of ethics; my parents-in-law, Daniel and Mary Ndetei, for fervent prayers and encouragement.
- The following friends for their prayers, encouragement and support during this study: Jack & Olivia Ranguma, Prof. Dan Kaseje, Hon. James Miruka-Owuor, Prof. Philip Mbithi, Eng. Jacqueline Musyoki, Daudi and Truphie Sumba, Nathan & Jane Chiroma, Mr. Michael Odote, Steve & Dianne Warn, Prof. James Kombo, and Rev. George Ouma.

PREFACE

THIS STUDY DESCRIBES AND analyzes the problem of termination of pregnancy, with special attention to its prevalence in Kenya, where more than seven hundred abortions are performed daily on girls between fifteen and seventeen years of age. Although pregnancy termination is illegal in Kenya, its practice goes on in the rural villages, in homes, in urban streets and in private clinics. The book focuses on the ethical quest for human dignity in the context of the church's response to the challenge of termination of pregnancy. It examines the perceptions and attitudes of various cadres of Christians, such as church ministers, doctors and lawyers, toward the problem. The study has been mainly through literature review of books, journals, magazines and newspapers, as well as through structured interviews and focus group discussions in Kisumu County of Kenya. Various viewpoints have been discussed and analyzed with regard to the problem. The book proposes Martin Benjamin's ethical theory of compromise as the most suitable means by which the church in Kenya can approach the challenge of termination of pregnancy. The theory finds support from Norman Geisler's theory of graded absolutism, as well as from a biblical analysis. Through the compromise theory, the book proposes that the church should lead in public advocacy for legalising pregnancy termination within the first six weeks of pregnancy in order to deal with pregnancies arising out of rape and incest. Findings from structured interviews and focused group discussions support the current legal framework that prohibits pregnancy termination, but reveal a desire for change in the way the church deals with members who get unplanned pregnancies and those who terminate the same. The book suggests, in addition, that the church's role should emphasize counseling, teaching and pastoral care, rather than excommunication and public rebuke. The church should avoid activism which seeks to keep abortion illegal at the expense of numerous Kenyans who do not necessarily submit to the church's position. Within the church, and among those whom the church seeks to convert, the author upholds the church's teaching of chastity and abstinence as the most effective preventive measures against abortion. The thesis proposes these measures as the means to ensuring human dignity within the church in relation to the ethical challenge of termination of pregnancy.

OPSOMMING

HIERDIE STUDIE BESKRYF EN ontleed die probleem van die beëindiging van swangerskap, met spesiale aandag aan die voorkoms daarvan in Kenia, waar meer as sewe-honderd aborsies daagliks uitgevoer word op meisies tussen vyftien en sewentien jaar oud. Hoewel swangerskap-beëindiging onwettig is in Kenia, vind dit steeds plaas in die plattelandse dorpies, in huise, in stedelike strate en in private klinieke. Die navorsing fokus op die etiese strewe na menswaardigheid in die lig van die kerk se reaksie op die uitdaging van die beëindiging van swangerskap. Dit ondersoek die persepsies en houdings van verskillende kaders van Christene, soos predikante, dokters en prokureurs, ten opsigte van die probleem. Die studie is hoofsaaklik gedoen deur 'n literatuuroorsig van boeke, artikels, koerante en tydskrifte, sowel as deur middel van gestruktureerde onderhoude en fokus-groep besprekings in die distrik van Kisumu, Kenia. Verskillende standpunte word bespreek en ontleed met betrekking tot die probleem.

Die navorsing stel Martin Benjamin se etiese teorie van kompromie voor as die mees geskikte manier waarop die kerk in Kenia die uitdaging van die beëindiging van swangerskap kan benader. Die teorie word ondersteun deur Norman Geisler se teorie van gegradeerde absolutisme sowel as deur 'n Bybelse analise. Deur die kompromie-teorie stel die navorsing voor dat die kerk leiding moet neem in openbare voorspraak vir die wettiging van swangerskap-beëindiging binne die eerste ses weke van swangerskappe wat voortspruit uit verkragting en bloedskande. Bevindinge van gestruktureerde onderhoude en gefokusde groepbesprekings ondersteun die huidige regsraamwerk wat swangerskap-beëindiging verbied, maar openbaar 'n begeerte vir 'n verandering in die manier waarop die kerk optree teenoor lede wat onbeplan swanger raak en diegene wat aborsies kry. Die navorsing dui

Opsomming

verder daarop dat die kerk se rol eerder moet fokus op berading, onderrig en pastorale sorg, as op ekskommunikasie en openbare teregwysing. Die kerk moet aktivisme vermy wat poog om aborsie onwettig te hou ten koste van die talle Keniane wat hulle nie noodwendig aan die kerk onderwerp nie. Binne die kerk, en onder diegene wat die kerk wil bekeer, ondersteun die navorser die kerk se lering van kuisheid en onthouding as die mees doeltreffende voorkomende maatreëls teen aborsie. Die tesis stel hierdie maatreëls voor as middele om menswaardigheid, met betrekking tot die etiese uitdaging van die beëindiging van swangerskap, binne die kerk te verseker.

ABBREVIATIONS

ACC	Area Church Council
AIC	Africa Inland Church
AIDS	Acquired Immuno-Deficiency Syndrome
AMECEA	Association of Member Episcopal Churches in Eastern Africa
CCC	Central Church Council
DCC	District Church Council
FGD	Focus Group Discussions
GLUK	Great Lakes University of Kisumu
GREC	Great Lakes University of Kisumu Research Ethics Committee
LCC	Local Church Council
RCC	Regional Church Council
WHO	World Health Organisation

CHAPTER 1

THE SIGNIFICANT CHALLENGE OF PREGNANCY TERMINATION

MOTIVATION FOR THE STUDY

In August 2010 Kenya officially promulgated a new constitution in which termination of pregnancy was clearly stated as illegal, and life was defined as beginning from the point of conception. This conclusion was reached as a compromise because the church in Kenya had clearly threatened to mobilize their members against voting in support of the new constitution in the referendum. Since 1990, over the years in which the political leadership of the country has agitated for constitutional change that would restructure governance and resource distribution, women's reproductive rights has come up in the discussions, as gynecologists propose that termination of pregnancy be legalized. Every time the topic has come up, church leaders have strongly defended the illegality of abortion, consistently declaring it as murder.

The challenge the country now faces is that, while termination of pregnancy remains illegal, women obtain abortion services form illegal clinics that are often managed by unqualified staff. The common result is that many lives of such women are lost; those who remain alive have complications that make their lives unhealthy and painful. The church in

Kenya continues to stand as a strong voice against the legalization of abortion in Kenya, while a significant number of women, including Christians, continue to suffer ill reproductive health and loss of life as a result of illegally procured abortion. The legislation processes continue to respect the church's opinion and retains the illegal status of abortion.

Women who procure abortion are placed on church discipline, including excommunication, the fear of which leads to much secrecy among women faced with the problem of abortion. The significance of this problem is seen in the loss of human dignity among women of reproductive age due to the stigmatization they face both in the church and in the society. The stigmatization is sustained by the government through its failure to provide legal and administrative structures for intervention. Similarly, the church, in its failure to prioritize human life and dignity over theological and moral dogma, contributes to the stigmatization.

The approach of the church to the ethical problem of abortion, through discipline, excommunication and public condemnation, perpetuates stigmatization and loss of human dignity. This approach is a problem in the world today, especially in Kenya, thereby making it necessary to study and evaluate in light of the theological-ethical teachings of the Reformation.

BACKGROUND OF THE STUDY

Abortion was a silent problem in Kenya until November 1998 when the Ministry of Education released an official statement indicating that an average of seven hundred abortions were performed daily in the country on girls between fifteen and seventeen years of age.[1] At that time, ten thousand girls were dropping out of school every year on account of unwanted pregnancies. Over a quarter million abortion cases are carried out annually. The editorial of the *Sunday Standard* commented with concern: "Of course it is known where abortions are performed in Kenya, but you do not hear of arrests being made, let alone prosecutions being pursued. The law looks the other way."[2] In August 1999 the then permanent secretary in the Ministry of Health, Prof. Julius Meme, suggested that the abortion problem needed to be debated with a view to licensing it. A day later, he withdrew his statement and reaffirmed the government's official position

---

1. *Sunday Standard*, 8 November 1998, 6.
2. Ibid.

that "abortion would stay illegal, except if the mother's life was in danger.[3] This sparked off a public debate in which a number of physicians called for the legalization of abortion, while others equated such a move with the legalization of murder. For the months that followed, the religious community, especially Christians, argued strongly against any attempts to legalize abortion. On 26 May 2004 residents of an estate in Nairobi woke up to find fifteen aborted fetuses wrapped in a polythene bag and dumped beneath a bridge on the Ngong' River.[4] In recent years, between 2002 and 2010, whenever Kenyans discussed the need for a new constitution, the church maintained that termination of pregnancy must remain illegal if Christians were to support the new constitution. The churches in Kenya have consistently done this through public statements by their leaders in the national groups like the National Council of Churches of Kenya, the Evangelical Alliance, the Organization of African Independent Churches, as well as the Roman Catholic Church.

Termination of pregnancy is, at the time of this study, both unconstitutional and illegal in Kenya. The Constitution of Kenya expressly prohibits it in the Bill of Rights. Part 2 of Article 26 of the Constitution further states that the life of a person shall begin at conception. Part 4 of the same article gives exceptions in the statement: "Abortion is not permitted unless, in the opinion of a trained health professional, there is need for emergency treatment, or the life or health of the mother is in danger, or if permitted by any other written law."[5] The currently existing and functioning provisions of the penal code, as last amended in 1973 (Sections 158–60), generally prohibit abortion:

> Any person who, with intent to procure the miscarriage of a woman, unlawfully administers to her any noxious thing or uses any other means is subject to 14 years' imprisonment. A woman who undertakes the same act with respect to herself or consents to it is subject to seven years' imprisonment. Any person who supplies

---

3. "Abortion Stays Illegal," *Daily Nation*, 14 August 1999.

4. "My Health," *Standard*, 6 March 2012, 5.

5. The Constitution of Kenya, 2010, 24. Article 24, Part 4 should be read carefully together with Article 43, Part 1(a) which states that "every person has the right to the highest attainable standard of health, which includes the right to health care services, including reproductive health care." Although termination of pregnancy is prohibited in the former, the phrase "reproductive health care" in the latter may be interpreted to include medical indications for termination, as well as post-abortion care in licensed medical facilities.

anything knowing that it is intended to be unlawfully used to procure a miscarriage is subject to three years' imprisonment.[6]

Nonetheless, under other provisions of the penal code an abortion may be performed to save the life of a pregnant woman. Section 240 of the code provides that a person is not criminally responsible for performing, in good faith and with reasonable care and skill, a surgical operation upon an unborn child for the preservation of the mother's life if the performance of the operation is reasonable having regard to the patient's state at the time, and to all the circumstances of the case. In view of the strict provisions of the law in Kenya, the termination of pregnancy takes place in private clinics, rural villages, and informal (unlicensed) clinics. Past medical investigations in Kenya revealed that, every day, there were more than 1,500 hospital admissions for complications from unsafe abortions carried out in the back streets by untrained personnel.[7] Abortion remains prevalent despite its illegal status in Kenya, and the society is divided on whether to legalize it or not.

Abortion is not merely a Kenyan or an African problem, but a global one. In the Western world, for instance, where abortion has been largely legalized, the problem is increasing instead of decreasing. This is especially so in the United States, Norway, and the Netherlands. Payne reports that since 1973, when the famous Roe versus Wade case was passed and abortion effectively legalized, thirty million induced abortions have taken place in the United States.[8] In Africa the practice has been legalized in Zambia, South Africa, and Burundi, with a few countries seeking to follow suit. But in the rest of the continent, abortion remains largely illegal. Unplanned and unwanted pregnancy is the main driving force behind the increasing

---

6. In practice, there is a relationship between Kenya's legal tradition and that of Britain, its former colonizer, as discussed on p. 87 of the Population Policy Data Bank (2011) maintained by the Population Division of the Department for Economic and Social Affairs of the United Nations Secretariat. The document cites an example where Kenya like a number of Commonwealth countries, whose legal systems are based on English common law, follows the holding of the 1938 English *Rex v. Bourne* decision in determining whether an abortion performed for health reasons is lawful. In the *Bourne* decision, a physician was acquitted of the offence of performing an abortion in the case of a woman who had been raped. The court ruled that the abortion was lawful because it had been performed to prevent the woman from becoming "a physical and mental wreck," thus setting a precedent for future abortion cases performed on the grounds of preserving the pregnant woman's physical and mental health.

7. Lema et al., "Induced Abortion in Kenya," 164.

8. Payne, *Biblical Healing for Modern Medicine*, 107.

practice of abortion among both married and unmarried couples who are sexually active. Even where a qualified medical doctor or gynecologist terminates a pregnancy, there have been negative physical, psychological and emotional consequences.

While medical practitioners and lawyers have been evenly divided on the merits and demerits of legalizing abortion, the church in Kenya has firmly and unanimously opposed any proposed legalization of the practice. Apparently, the approach of the church on the problem of abortion remains dominant and influential in public debate, and directly influences the outcome of public policy and legislation. In view of the foregoing situation, a critical evaluation is necessary on the church's approach to the ethical challenge of abortion in order to use Reformation theology to make recommendations for the church.

STATEMENT OF THE PROBLEM

The church continues to stand against the legalization of abortion in Kenya, while a significant number of women continue to suffer ill reproductive health and loss of life as a result of illegally procured abortion. The legislation organs and processes continue to respect and uphold the church's opinion, thus affirming and retaining the illegal status of abortion. Women who procure abortion are placed on public church discipline, including excommunication, the fear of which leads to much secrecy among women faced with unplanned pregnancies. This approach of the church perpetuates stigmatization and loss of human dignity through public discipline and excommunication, thereby making it necessary to study and evaluate in light of the theological ethics.

MAGNITUDE OF THE PROBLEM OF PREGNANCY TERMINATION

Statistics from Africa

Recent research carried out by the Guttmacher Institute on the overall abortion rate in Africa, where the vast majority of abortions are illegal and unsafe, showed no decline between 2003 and 2008, holding at 29 abortions per 1,000 women of childbearing age. The report noted that the Southern Africa subregion, dominated by South Africa, where abortion was legalized in 1997, has the lowest abortion rate of all African subregions, at 15 per 1,000 women in 2008. East Africa has the highest rate, at 38, followed by Middle Africa at 36, West Africa at 28 and North Africa at 1.[9] In terms of estimated numbers, Nondo E. Ejano of the Women Promotion Centre in Kigoma, Tanzania, reports that the annual number of induced abortions in Africa rose from 5.0 million to 5.6 million between 1995 and 2003. In 2003, most of the abortions occurred in Eastern Africa (2.3 million), Western Africa (1.5 million), and Northern Africa (1 million). Kenya is part of East Africa, where the rates are highest at 39 abortions per 1,000 women aged 15–44. In Tanzania, abortion complications contributed 18% of maternal deaths in 2008.[10] In Uganda, each year, an estimated 297,000 induced abortions are performed, and nearly 85,000 women are treated for complications. Abortions occur at a rate of 54 per 1,000 women aged 15–49 and account for one in five pregnancies.[11]

Fred Sai's earlier research reported that every year between 30 and 60 million women in the world sought termination of pregnancy. It was estimated that about 500,000 women died every year due to induced abortion unsafely performed. This figure was about 50% of maternal deaths around the world. In Africa alone at least 150,000 women lost their lives through pregnancy and related causes each year; of these 25% to 50% died because of unsafely induced abortion. In Zimbabwe, about 28% of maternal deaths were abortion related, while Tanzania and Ethiopia had 21% and 54% respectively.[12]

In the Republic of South Africa, where termination of pregnancy has been legal since 1997, Robert Johnston reports that there were 68,736 abortion cases reported from various health facilities throughout the country in 2008.[13] Earlier, in 1989, it had been estimated that there were 43,000 abortions, out of which 42,000 were legal while 1,000 were illegal. There were six abortions in every 1,000 women aged 15 to 40. Between 1979 and 1984, 124 abortions were performed yearly at Groote Schuur Hospital in Cape Town. This represented 30% of legal abortions before reproductive health laws were fully liberalized in South Africa in 1997. Between June 1992 and

9. Guttmacher, "Facts on Induced Abortion Worldwide," 2.
10. Ejano, *Tanzania: Unsafe Abortion*, 1.
11. Singh et al., "Incidence of Induced Abortion in Uganda."
12. Sai, "Overview of Unsafe Abortion in Africa," 2.
13. Johnston, "Historical Abortion Statistics, South Africa."

July 1993, 331 of the 502 applications for abortion on psychiatric grounds at Groote Schuur Hospital were approved.[14]

According to reports from Guttmacher Institute, abortion is illegal in Nigeria except to save a woman's life, is common, and most procedures are performed under unsafe, clandestine conditions. In 1996, an estimated 610,000 abortions occurred (25 per 1,000 women of childbearing age), of which 142,000 resulted in complications severe enough to require hospitalization. The number of abortions was estimated to have risen to 760,000 in 2006. Unsafe abortions were a major reason Nigeria's maternal mortality rate—1,100 deaths per 100,000 live births—was one the highest in the world. According to conservative estimates, more than 3,000 women die annually in Nigeria as a result of unsafe abortion.[15]

It was reported that nearly half of the population of West Africa and one quarter of Africa's population lives in Nigeria.[16] Although induced abortion rates among schoolgirls were high in Lagos, Nigeria, 34.8% of the women who underwent abortions were married women, and 52.2% were women with two or more children. In 1987, it was estimated that half the female population in Liberia between the ages of 14 and 21 who were currently attending school had had an induced abortion. Adolescent girls who were enrolled in school formed 60% of the 1,489 patients treated for complications resulting from unsafe abortion.[17]

Similar studies by Khama O. Rogo reveal that most abortion studies in Africa are hospital based, and according to most hospital records the number of victims of unsafe abortion had been rising rapidly in the last two decades. Rogo recounts that an average of forty cases were now seen daily at Kenyatta National Hospital in Nairobi, indicating an increase of between 600% and 800% over the preceding decade. Similar observations were reported from Lusaka and Kinshasa where, as in Nairobi, more than 60% of the cases were most likely induced.[18]

In East and Central Africa, according to Rogo, at least 20% of all maternal deaths were due to complications of induced abortion. In Ethiopia, a community-based study estimated the proportion at 54% of all maternal deaths. In West African studies, very rarely had abortion accounted for

14. Benatar, "Abortion: Some Practical and Ethical Considerations," 469.
15. Guttmacher, "Reducing Unsafe Abortion in Nigeria."
16. Emuveyan, "Profile of Abortion in Nigeria," 8.
17. Sai, "Overview of Unsafe Abortion," 3.
18. Rogo et al., "Induced Abortion in Sub-Saharan Africa," 15.

more than 10% of maternal deaths.[19] It was yet to be established whether this may have been because abortion was safer in West than East Africa, or that the prevalence of other causes of maternal mortality (such as sepsis and hemorrhage) was disproportionately high in West Africa. It is also possible that the influence of conservative Islam is a deterrent factor hindering many potential abortion cases from taking place.

From these statistics it is logical to conclude that illegally induced abortions significantly contribute to maternal mortality in Africa. It appears that where there are illegal abortions being carried out, safe abortions are likely to be inaccessible to the poor, and may become a privilege for a limited number of women. From the number of post-abortion hospital admissions it seems that most illegal abortions are incomplete due to either inadequate training of the personnel involved or lack of proper equipment and anesthesia. This raises concern for the many human lives lost due to illegal abortion, and forms a basis for seeking to legalize the practice, on the assumption that legalized abortion will reduce abortion-related deaths. However, it is the argument of this research that statistics of deaths caused by abortion cannot be independently used to seek a legal status for the practice. Ethical issues involved must be considered as well, for in theological ethics, what is legal is not always necessarily morally right.

Statistics from Kenya

In Kenya some people are in favor of legalized abortion because of the concerns about the negative effects of backstreet abortion. The argument is that, since illegal abortions are leading to deaths and health risks, safe abortion needs to be made readily available. But it can also be argued that, just because something might happen anyway is not a good enough reason for the Kenyan society to legalize it. The exact number of illegal unsafe abortions in Kenya is not known, since by their very nature, illegal abortions are not registered in official statistics. They are, however, estimated from hospital in-patient records, survey data, birth rate analysis and maternal mortality statistics.

According to recent research done by the East Africa Centre for Law and Justice, there were about 310,000 abortions every year in Kenya. Twenty-one thousand women were admitted each year due to abortion-related complications, usually done in backstreet clinics. Two thousand six

19. Ibid.

hundred of these eventually died. Of the women admitted, 12% were older than 34, 40% were between 25 and 34, while 16% were teenagers.[20] One of the key challenges noted by the East Africa Centre for Law and Justice in this phenomenon is the rise of abortion-related complications which get attention in health facilities.

> Only 16% of delivery institutions can perform the vacuum aspiration procedure, which uses suction to empty the uterus and is the preferred method recommended by the WHO (World Health Organization). Women in rural areas have much less access to treatment as compared to those in urban settings. Also, it is private facilities that handle more than half of post abortion cases, yet they charge three times more than the public sector facilities.[21]

The treatment of post-abortion cases remains at a high, despite the attempt by health facilities to treat them in time. Onyango et al., in their study to establish the national magnitude of unsafe abortion, reported that almost one in five post-abortion cases arrived at the hospital in critical condition, and one out of every ten arrived with organ failure.[22] As such, maternal morbidity remains remarkably high in Kenya.

In an earlier study it was found that 46% of abortion patients had between one and three children, 21.8% had between four and six children, and 7% had seven children or more. It was estimated that there were at least 112,500 spontaneous and 75,000 induced abortions in 1990. This represented an induced abortion rate of 15 for every 1,000 women (15 to 49 years) or one abortion for every 100 pregnancies. Rogo's extrapolation of this for the whole continent gave estimates of 1.5 million induced abortions by 1990. The study also established that only 58 legal abortions were performed at Kenyatta National Hospital over a period of 4 years, in contrast to the 30 to 40 daily admissions of illegally induced abortions.[23] The main indicators for the few reported legal terminations were psychosocial problems which were interpreted by psychiatrists to be life threatening.

There are indications that some pregnancy terminations in Kenya occur under fairly safe conditions, since they are carried out by trained health staff illegally in private hospitals. It may be observed that

---

20. East Africa Centre for Law and Justice.
21. Ibid.
22. Onyango et al., "Scaling Up Access," 9.
23. Rogo et al., "Induced Abortion," 15.

the exact magnitude of the problem of illegally induced abortion in Kenya is unknown but the prevalence of infected, incomplete abortions indicate that such terminations are common. Case-control studies of illegal versus legal abortion would theoretically be attractive to distinguish risk factors for illegal abortion. In Kenya, however, legal abortion is not available on demand, and patients tend to deny clandestine interventions for fear of being prosecuted.[24]

It is quite instructive that abortions accounted for 5% of all hospital admissions and up to 50% of all gynecological admissions in Nairobi. Both induced and spontaneous abortions formed about 63% of the gynecological admissions into Kenyan hospitals. Of these, about 65% were thought to be induced illegally and unsafely.[25] Many other illegally induced abortions took place in the community, but these neither got documented nor reached hospitals. It seems that many women obtained illegal but clinically safe abortions, performed by doctors. Instructions given to such clients to go to the emergency ward without delay, should any complications be noted, tend to contribute to an underestimate of the true prevalence of clandestine abortions.

It was observed that, in Kenya, having an unwanted pregnancy was not mainly due to lack of knowledge of contraceptives. Rather, it was due to other factors, such as fear of side effects and unavailability of contraceptives.[26] It is possible that, if the provision of safe, legal abortions was made available, many human lives and lots of money would be saved. Any serious post-abortion complications normally have adverse economic repercussions for both the individual and the community. Although induced abortion permeates all social and economic strata in Kenya, it seems that certain categories of individuals are more at risk than others. It has been reported that induced unsafe abortion is more common among young, single women, schoolgirls and those in urban settings.[27]

24. Sjostrand et al., "Socio-Economic Client Characteristics," 325.
25. Ibid., 326.
26. Ibid., 322.
27. Lema et al., "Induced Abortion in Kenya," 164.

PURPOSE OF THE STUDY

The church in Kenya is capable of providing theologically informed and ethically suitable solutions and resolutions on the problem of abortion. The purpose of this study was to critically review the quest for human dignity in the ethical challenge of termination of pregnancy and to evaluate the church's approach in the light of theological ethics in order to make appropriate recommendations to the church.

RESEARCH OBJECTIVES

The research was designed to fulfill the following objectives:

1. To determine the human dignity issues in the ethical challenge of pregnancy termination.
2. To establish the approach of the Africa Inland Church (AIC) to the ethical problem of pregnancy termination.
3. To develop a viable theological-ethical theory applicable to the problem of pregnancy termination.
4. To determine the relationship between the church's approach to pregnancy termination and theological-ethical theory on the problem.
5. To make recommendations to the church based on the findings of the research.

RESEARCH QUESTIONS

The study set out aiming at providing answers to the following questions:

1. How does termination of pregnancy relate to the quest for human dignity in theological ethics?
2. In what ways does the AIC church in Kenya approach the ethical problem of pregnancy termination?
3. What theological-ethical theory should the AIC church adopt to resolve the problem of pregnancy termination?
4. How should a suitable theological-ethical theory influence the church's approach to pregnancy termination?

5. How does the theological-ethical theory relate to human dignity in termination of pregnancy?
6. What recommendations can the study make to the church, based on the findings of the research?

RATIONALE FOR THE STUDY

This study expresses its value in seeking to enhance the AIC church's ability to make theologically informed contributions in educating its members in particular, and the public in general, on the ethical concerns in abortion. In this research, the researcher expresses the Christian pastoral concern over the problem of abortion as it affects human dignity and livelihood. The research also enhances the church's ability to contribute to the endeavors in search of resolutions to the ethical problem of abortion. It is intended that the churches in Kenya will directly benefit from the study and adopt the suggestions made herein in order to formulate clear moral guidelines for their members. Such moral guidelines may be published in manuals, not as rulebooks, but as resource material for priests and pastors involved in theological discourse, catechumen and pastoral counseling in the churches. In seeking solutions to the problem, this research indulges the teachings of the Reformed tradition.

ASSUMPTIONS OF THE STUDY

While undertaking the study, the researcher made the following assumptions:

1. The discussions and responses from documents and reports give an accurate representation of the denominational positions of various churches in Kenya.
2. The responses from the selected AIC church leaders and members accurately represent the general population in the Christian community in Kenya in general, and the AIC in particular.
3. The church's future approach to abortion can integrate human dignity based on a study of a theological-ethical evaluation of the problem.

4. Recommendations from the study can apply to the church in general and specific denominations in particular.

LIMITATIONS AND DELIMITATIONS OF THE RESEARCH

In appreciation of the magnitude of the subject under study, this research has the following limitations:

1. In view of the universal occurrence of abortion, the study is limited to the Kenyan context. However, whenever it is relevant and possible, studies from other regions in the world are applied as well.
2. In the analysis and evaluation of discussions, attention focuses on the teachings of the Africa Inland Church, as well as the perceptions, attitudes and opinions of the church's leaders and members, with regard to the problem of pregnancy termination. Since the country of Kenya, as covered by the AIC, is practically too large to be studied effectively in this research, structured interviews and focused group discussions is done in selected AIC local churches of Nyanza Area.
3. Given the various forms of abortion that take place, including those professionally prescribed by physicians, this research is limited to elective induced abortion only.
4. Statistical data indicating the occurrences and effects of abortion are drawn from secondary sources. Since the researcher is neither a physician nor a psychiatrist, no deliberate effort is made to interview women who have had personal experiences with abortion. Instead, the research draws from what the experts in these fields have written.
5. Theological ethics are extensively studied and applied in analysis and evaluation, in addition to structured interviews and focused group discussions.

METHODOLOGY OF THE STUDY

The study involved an evaluation of written and reported discussions and responses from purposely chosen AIC local churches in Kisumu County, Nyanza Area. In each chosen local church group, there was a theological-ethical evaluation of statements from both the leaders and the members of the representative local church, taking gender composition into consideration. The study was primarily library-based and evaluative. This study has both primary data and secondary data. The primary data was collected from structured interviews, focused group discussions and church records. Secondary data was collected from newspaper reports, journal articles and books. In the structured interviews, intense qualitative probe questions were asked to the respondents. In addition, focused group discussions yielded information on opinions, feelings and attitudes of Christians on the problem of termination of pregnancy. The entire Nyanza Area has a total of 70 districts, 600 local churches, and a membership of about 18,000 Christians in total. This study focused on 10 local churches considered to be key or strategic, but carefully selected to represent the entire Nyanza Area. In each local church selected, a focused group was formed based on the existing church structure.

DEFINITION OF TERMS

In order to facilitate a clear understanding of the problem under research, it is necessary to provide definitions and explanations of key terms in the thesis title, namely, abortion and termination of pregnancy, ethics, as well as human dignity. Other terms used in the thesis may be defined either within the main text, in the footnotes, or in the glossary of terms.

Abortion and Termination of Pregnancy

Webster's New Twentieth Century Dictionary of the English Language defines abortion as "the act of miscarrying or producing young before the natural time, or before the fetus is perfectly formed: called criminal abortion when unlawful."[28] The *Oxford English Reference Dictionary* briefly states that abortion is "the expulsion of a fetus (naturally or by medical induction) from the womb before it is able to survive independently."[29] These definitions are grammatically useful in providing a basic understanding of the word in its common use, but give no clear distinction between deliberate acts of abortion and unfortunate miscarriages caused by ill health during

---

28. *Webster's New Twentieth Century Dictionary*, s.v. "abortion."
29. *Oxford English Reference Dictionary*, s.v. "abortion."

pregnancy. The *New Encyclopedia Britannica* offers more details and makes the distinction lacking in both Webster's and Oxford's dictionaries:

> The expulsion of a fetus from the uterus before it has reached the stage of viability (in human beings, usually about the twentieth week of gestation). An abortion may occur spontaneously, in which case it is called a miscarriage, or it may be brought on purposefully, in which case it is often called an induced abortion.[30]

Dr. Khama O. Rogo, a director of Nairobi's Centre for the Study of Adolescents and previous chairman of Kenya Medical Association, notes that abortion may be either spontaneous or induced.[31] Dr. John Nyamu, the executive director of Reproductive Health Services, in an interview with the *Sunday Nation Lifestyle*, defines abortion as "the termination of a pregnancy, for whatever reasons, before the twentieth week of gestation or before it reaches 500 grams weight."[32]

Theological ethical definitions, however, seem to be different, and include moral remarks. In a pastoral letter, the Catholic Bishops of Zambia define abortion as the termination of a pregnancy, either by miscarriage (spontaneous) or by intervention (induced) before the fetus is capable of surviving outside the womb.[33] They add that, morally, abortion is the direct and deliberate killing of unborn human life. To this the Catholic Bishops of Ethiopia and Eritrea add a more vivid description: "Abortion is the removal of the baby from the mother's womb before the fetus is fully grown and able to survive.... This is the deliberate, direct killing of the human being in the first phase of its life between conception and birth."[34]

A theologian of the evangelical persuasion, Millard J. Erickson, defines abortion as "an intentional act of terminating a pregnancy with the aim of bringing about the death of the fetus."[35] D. H. Field calls it "the loss or expulsion from the womb of a living fetus before it has reached the stage of viability."[36] Carl Horn III refers to it as "an induced termination of pregnancy in a manner designed to kill the embryo or fetus."[37] Byron C.

30. *New Encyclopedia Britannica*, s.v. "abortion."
31. Rogo et al., "Induced Abortion," 14.
32. "Safe Motherhood," *Sunday Nation*, 5 September 1999, 6.
33. ADS, 2/1998, no. 485, 2.
34. ADS, 9–10/1999, no. 501
35. Erickson, *Concise Dictionary of Christian Theology*, 9.
36. Field, "Abortion," 2.
37. Horn, "Abortion," 4.

Calhoun equates it murder: "Abortion is the wrongful taking of an unborn baby's life before birth ... in a premeditated and a ruthless manner."[38]

The expressions above lead to the conclusion that theological-ethically influenced definitions make strong moral statements on both the human status of the fetus and the equation of abortion to murder. A biomedical ethical study, such as this one, seeks to integrate both the medical definitions from physicians and the moral ones from the theologians. The two earlier definitions of the Catholic Bishops are adequate, except for the phrase "before the fetus is capable of surviving outside the womb." This phrase would need to be deleted from a theological ethical definition of abortion because some late-term abortions are carried out on babies capable of surviving, but who are then deliberately either killed or abandoned to die. Although such killing or abandonment ethically falls into the category of infanticide, the initial act that expels the baby from the womb is abortion. An integration of the Catholic Bishops' definition with that of Erickson would be a more viable one: Abortion is an intentional act of terminating a pregnancy between conception and birth, with the aim of deliberately bringing about the death of the fetus. A distinction is, however, made between abortion as defined above and indirect, therapeutic abortion where the intention is to cure an organ of the mother's body. For instance, physicians may need to remove a cancerous womb or an ectopic pregnancy that cannot develop, and in the process an indirect abortion becomes an unavoidable consequence.

Physicians make reference to safe and unsafe abortion. Unsafe abortion is defined as the interruption of pregnancy with less than optimal technology, counseling, emotional support, aftercare, and freedom of making informed decisions.[39] Where all these are available, abortion is said to be safe. Ramalefo and Modisaotsile report that legal abortion with the assistance of optimal technology is said to be safer than childbirth.[40] However, the medical accuracy of that statement is called into question by the negative psychological and physiological effects of abortion, including that done by physicians, as can be verified from findings enumerated within this research.

In this research, the terms termination of pregnancy and abortion will be used interchangeably in reference to the deliberate interruption of a

---

38. Calhoun, "Am I a Murderer?," 46.
39. Ramalefo and Modisaotsile, "State of Unsafe Abortion in Botswana," 38.
40. Ibid., 40.

pregnancy resulting in the expulsion of a fetus from the mother's womb in order to discontinue its life.

Ethics

The term *ethics* commonly refers to the study of standards of conduct and moral judgment, and is also known as moral philosophy; it also refers to the system or code of morals of a particular philosopher, group, or profession.[41] A similar definition is found in the *Oxford English Reference Dictionary*.[42] Erickson uses similar phrases to define ethics in the Christian context as "a system of right and wrong based upon Christian principles and teachings . . . the study of right and wrong based upon, or found in, the Bible."[43] Louis P. Pojman elaborates and describes ethics as

> the systematic endeavour to understand moral concepts and justify moral principles and theories. It undertakes to analyze such concepts as "right," "wrong," "permissible," "ought," "good," and "evil" in their moral contexts. It builds and scrutinizes arguments setting forth large-scale theories on how we ought to act.[44]

The etymology of the word is of prime value in helping the reader to obtain a clear understanding of the concept of ethics, and the *Theological Dictionary of the New Testament* is hereby found quite helpful. The English noun comes from the Greek word *ethikos*, which means, "arising from use or custom." The more basic term from which *ethikos* is derived is *ethos*, which signifies use, habit, custom, manner, cultic ordinance, or law.[45]

In the Old Testament the term generally refers to Jewish laws and regulations of worship. In Luke 22:39, *ethos* is used to explain that it was Jesus' custom to stay on the Mount of Olives for prayers whenever he was in Jerusalem. This was a religious habit, which Jesus did not take over from the religious community but adopted for himself. In Acts 25:16 *ethos* denotes the custom of Roman justice that the accused be confronted by his accusers and be granted the chance to defend himself. In Hebrews 10:25 the word is used in the context of the censure of a bad custom or habit

---

41. Webster, s.v. "ethics."
42. *Oxford English Reference Dictionary*, s.v. "ethics."
43. Erickson, *Concise Dictionary of Christian Theology*, 51.
44. Pojman, *Ethical Theory*, 1.
45. Kittel, *Theological Dictionary of the New Testament*, 373.

of non-attendance of the assembly of believers. In the Jewish understanding, *ethos* expresses the faithfulness and constancy of God, and provides the basis upon which human beings display a dignity and solemnity commensurate with the divine majesty. It is clear from the proceeding that the word *ethics* originated in the customs and habits of groups, to which their members were expected to adhere.

The term *ethics*, according to Jay E. Adams (1987:20), refers to

> the standards of conduct adopted by a group or individual as a discipline; it is the study of moral values belonging to such groups or persons. . . . It is a plural noun when it means a system of moral principles, but singular when used to denote the field or discipline, which studies such matters.[46]

Within this understanding, the expression "biomedical ethics" is used to describe those standards under which physicians, nurses, and other medical personnel conduct themselves when carrying out medical practice. However, such standards may not be universal and, therefore, have inherent problems on those who seek to abide by them. Adams observes that

> the problem with this concept of ethics deeply embodied in both the word and its history is that human beings set standards according to the values that they accept. There is no objective, universal standard of moral persons for all time and in every culture. . . . These codes are, therefore, subject to change according to the whims of society and the biases of the majority of the persons subscribing to them.[47]

In light of the foregoing discussions, it is reasonable to agree with Morris A. Inch, who defines ethics as "the enquiry into man's moral nature so as to discover what are his responsibilities and the means by which he may fulfill them."[48] Inch discusses his definition further in order to provide a more adequate understanding:

> The field of ethical enquiry can be divided into philosophical, theological and Christian ethics. Philosophical ethics approaches man's responsibility from what can be known by natural reason and in respect to temporal existence. Theological ethics deals with

---

46. Adams, "What Are/Is Christian Ethics?," 20.
47. Ibid.
48. Inch, "Ethics," 375.

what may be gained from the alleged insight of any given religious community as to this life or that to come. Christian ethics is the Christian instance of theological ethics.[49]

In this research, the term *theological ethics* is used in its narrow sense to refer specifically to Christian ethics, in which basic biblical and theological principles are integrated with resultant ethical principles to evaluate the various perspectives on termination of pregnancy. The writer, however, does not exclude philosophical ethical approaches in this process, but evaluates them from a Christian viewpoint. Scripture and theology helps in creating an understanding of the difference between good and evil in biomedical theological ethics.

Human Dignity

According to Mette Lebech, the English expression "human dignity" consists of the predicate "human" and the noun "dignity."[50] When "human"

---

49. Ibid.

50. Lebech, "What Is Human Dignity?," 1. Professor Lebech is a professor of Philosophy at the Faculty of Philosophy at the National University of Ireland. In this article, he gives linguistic clarity to the term as follows: "The adjective qualifies the noun, thus determining the kind of dignity in question as the human kind. The adjective has a similar function in the expression 'human being': Here it qualifies the noun 'being,' to determine the kind of being in question as a being of the human kind. 'Human' is etymologically related to the Latin for earth, *humus*, so that 'human' means what is 'earthly' (as an adjective), or an 'earthling' (as a substantive). Generally speaking it means what is proper to the kind that 'we' are, or to the species of rational animals, referring in particular to their kindness (humanity) and their fallibility ('all too human'). 'Dignity' comes from the Latin noun *decus*, meaning ornament, distinction, honour, glory. *Decet* is the verbal form (which is impersonal), and is related to the Greek δοκειν—to seem or to show. The Latin participle form decens, -tis, has survived in the English language in the adjective 'decent.' But dignity means, generally speaking, the standing of one entitled to respect, i.e., his or her status, and it refers to that which in a being (in particular a personal being) induces or ought to induce such respect: its excellence or incomparability of value. Paradoxically, *dignitas* translated the Greek αχιομα, when Latin was adapted so as to deal with logic, thus indicating that dignity, despite its 'showiness,' is really something to be taken for granted, like a first principle. *Dignitas* is understood to be self-imposing, important by virtue of itself; and even if it relies on something else that has given it, or that guarantees its status, it is understood to impose *itself*, in and through the authority given. As it cannot be reduced to what founds it, it is indeed comparable to an axiom, which must be taken for granted. *Dignitas* therefore is, with a neologism, a 'δοχα αχιοματικη,' something taught to be first, a highest value."

and "dignity" are used in conjunction they form the expression "human dignity," which means the status of human beings entitling them to respect, a status which is first and foremost to be taken for granted. It refers to their highest value, or to the fact that they are a presupposition for value, as they are those to whom value makes sense.

Lebech further proposes that the *idea* of human dignity conceptualizes or embraces this experience of recognition, and the *principle* of human dignity is the affirmation that the experience is possible in relation to all human beings. When formulated, the principle affirms the fundamental value of every human beings as such. It enjoys general acceptance all round the globe as a basic ethical and legal principle because it draws upon the universal experience of the dynamics of recognition. It clearly is in everyone's interest to be respected as having human dignity, i.e., as having the highest value due to an inalienable humanity.

In agreement with Lebech's foregoing discourse, the term "human dignity" can be used in moral, ethical and political discussions to signify that a human being has innate right to respect and ethical treatment. In ordinary usage it denotes respect and status, and is often used in the human context to suggest the need for one to receive a proper degree of respect, or even that one needs to treat oneself with proper self-respect.

The Constitution of Kenya considers human dignity as a foundational ingredient of the lives of citizens. The Bill of Rights states clearly in Section 28 on Human Dignity that "every person has inherent dignity and the right to have that dignity respected and protected."[51] Apparently, all the other freedoms guaranteed by the Kenyan Constitution derive their meaning from this one foundational statement, a principle reflected in other contemporary constitutional drafts.[52] In 1998, the United Nations mentioned dignity in the *UNESCO Declaration on the Human Genome and Human Rights*. At Article 2, the declaration states, "Everyone has a right to respect for their dignity." At Article 24, the declaration warns that treating a person to remove a genetic defect "could be contrary to human dignity." The commentary that accompanies the declaration says that, as a consequence of

---

51. Constitution of Kenya, 26.

52. See Currie and De Waal, "Human Dignity," 272–79. In the South African Constitution, "human dignity" is listed as one of the founding values of the South African state. Furthermore, the Bill of Rights is described as affirming the "democratic values of human dignity, equality and freedom." Section 10 of the Constitution, like the Kenyan one, explicitly states that "everyone has inherent dignity and the right to have their dignity respected and protected."

the possibility of germ-line treatment, "it is the very dignity of the human race which is at stake."[53]

In Christian theological dogma, the dignity of the human person is rooted in his or her creation in the image and likeness of God as stated in Genesis 1:26–27.[54] Since God deserves honor and respect, his special creature that directly bears his image also deserves honor and respect. The dignity of human beings is divine in origin, and is above situational contexts. From this doctrine individual human beings derive the right to exercise freedom.

The usage of the term "human dignity" in the context of this research makes reference to the right of human beings to exercise freedom because they are created in the image and likeness of God, besides the fact that the same right is guaranteed in national constitutions and international corporate organizations. With regard to the ethical challenge of termination of pregnancy, the research will endeavor to establish the persistent gap between definitive doctrinal statements and constitutional guarantees on the one hand, and practices that continue to alienate women from exercising freedom based on church doctrine and constitutional provisions. The research, while recognizing the rights of both the pregnant woman and the fetus to human dignity in terms of respect, honor, and value, will further endeavor to develop and propose a convergent ethical theory as a foundation for dealing with the challenges of termination of pregnancy.

Summary

This chapter has dealt with background of the study, research objectives and questions, as well as the definitions of key terms and concepts. Having established the ground for the research, it is now appropriate, in the next chapter, to turn to a review of available literature in the subject of research in order to understand the problem in historical, biblical and theological-ethical perspectives.

---

53. *UNESCO Declaration on the Human Genome and Human Rights*, Articles 2 and 24.

54. Gen 1:26–27 NIV: "Then God said, 'Let us make man in our image, in our likeness, and let them rule over the fish of the sea and the birds of the air, over the livestock, over all the earth, and over all the creatures that move along the ground.' So God created man in his image, in the image of God he created him; male and female he created them."

CHAPTER 2

HISTORICAL, BIBLICAL AND THEOLOGICAL-ETHICAL PERSPECTIVES ON TERMINATION OF PREGNANCY

INTRODUCTION

This chapter seeks to develop an understanding of the problem of termination of pregnancy, through a review of available literature, from historical, biblical and theological-ethical perspectives. The objective here is to enable the reader to appreciate the problem as has been discussed, debated and resolved in other contexts, and to identify the gaps that has left the problem largely unresolved, especially in the Kenyan context.

HISTORICAL PERSPECTIVES ON TERMINATION OF PREGNANCY

The earliest recorded reference of people carrying out abortion was in Chinese literature in 3,500 BC.[1] References in ancient texts of Greece and the Roman Empire indicate that contraception, abortion and the killing

---

1. Hurry, "Termination of Pregnancy," 20.

of an infant soon after birth, with the mother's consent, were frequently practiced.[2] According to the third-century BC Greek author Kleicharchos, fulfillment of a vow to a deity was probably the most frequent reason an infant or child was sacrificed.[3] It is also reported that deformed or unwanted female babies were often abandoned to die in ancient Greece and Rome.[4] Hippocrates, a physician in ancient Greece who did not agree with his contemporary Plato, wrote an oath in which he promised in part: "I will give no deadly medicine to anyone if asked . . . and in like manner I will not give a woman a pessary to produce an abortion."[5] Hippocrates was trying to reform the medical practices of his day. Hurry notes that abortion does not appear to have been condemned in the ancient Greco-Roman world and that some writers such as Aristotle and Socrates thought of abortion as a method of population control. Evidently, the Greco-Roman culture within which the early church had to live out its faith, tolerated, if not encouraged, both abortion and infanticide.[6] This church, then, had to vigorously and consistently make known its opposition to the taking of life in the womb. *The Didache* or *Teachings of the Twelve Apostles*, a manual of Christian principles that dates back to the first century, clearly prohibits abortion. In Didache 2:2, it is stated, "Thou shalt not procure abortion, nor commit infanticide," and "Thou shalt not slay a child by abortion."[7] The first-century *Epistle of Barnabas*, usually attributed by Bible scholars to Paul's missionary companion, states in the fifth verse of its nineteenth chapter, "You shall not destroy your conception before they are brought forth, not kill them after they are born."[8]

In the second-century Roman Empire, Christians were accused of being "homicides and devourers of men" due to the society's misunderstanding of the concept of the Eucharist. This charge of cannibalism and infanticide drew responses from Quintus Tertullian and Athenagoras, both second-century church fathers. Tertullian, a lawyer by profession, wrote his *Apology* to the Roman emperor, and defended Christians saying,

---

2. Ibid.
3. White, "Abortion and the Ancient Practice of Child Sacrifice," 34.
4. Grassian, *Moral Reasoning*, 246.
5. Fowler, *Abortion*, 18.
6. Hurry, "Termination of Pregnancy," 20.
7. Davis, *Abortion and the Christian*, 4.
8. Davis and Denney, *Time for Compassion*, 55.

> For us to whom murder has been once for all forbidden, it is not permitted to destroy even what has been conceived. To forbid birth is only quicker murder. It makes no difference whether one take away the life once born or destroy it as it comes to birth. He is a man who is to be a man. The fruit is always present in the seed.[9]

Tertullian, in affirming the moral evil of abortion said, "You shall not kill the embryo by abortion and shall not cause the new born to perish."[10] Tertullian is, however, reported to have considered a direct threat to the life of the mother to be a justifiable ground for abortion.[11] Athenagoras, a philosopher, also made his defense to Emperor Marcus Aurelius, in AD 177, in a similar manner:

> How can we kill a man when we are those who say that all who use abortifacients are homicides and will account to God for their abortions as for the killing of men. For the fetus in the womb is not an animal, and it is God's providence that he exists.[12]

Caesarius of Arles said, "No woman should take any drug to procure an abortion because she will be placed before the judgment seat of Christ whether she has killed an already born child or a conceived one."[13] Clement of Alexandria, in the second century AD, was even stronger in his choice of words: "Those women who conceal sexual wantonness by taking stimulating drugs to bring on an abortion wholly lose their humanity along with the fetus." Abortion was also condemned by Canon 61 of the Council of Elvira in the year 306 AD.[14]

The early Christian view of abortion is seen by Grassian to have been greatly influenced by Aristotelian metaphysics. Aristotle believed that a body possessed a human soul when it was capable of performing the functions that were unique to human beings, and that this was only possible when a body possessed a human shape and human organs, which were not clearly discernible in the fetus. To him an immature human fetus

---

9. Ibid.
10. ADS 9–10, no. 501, 3.
11. Davis, *Abortion and the Christian*, 4.
12. Ibid.
13. Fowler, *Abortion*, 17.

14 Cross, *Oxford Dictionary of the Christian Church*, 6 and 454. The Council of Elvira was a Spanish council of the church held just after a period of persecution. It passed 81 canons with severe disciplinary penalties enforced for apostasy. Punishment for those who broke the canon included lifelong excommunication even at death.

possessed a vegetative or animal soul, but not a human soul.[15] Aristotle and Socrates are reported to have thought of abortion as a method of population control.[16] Not all abortions were considered equally sinful. Both Augustine and Jerome believed that the destruction of the fetus could not be considered homicide until the fetus had fully formed. Full formation was achieved at ensoulment, and this only became a reality on the fortieth day for a male and eightieth day for a female following conception.[17] However, while Augustine was not certain about the exact time of ensoulment, he unreservedly condemned abortion as a practice. He viewed abortion as an expression of "lustful cruelty" and condemned "pagans who procured poisons of sterility (possibly a reference to contraceptives) . . . which would lead to the destruction of the fetus in the womb."[18]

This attitude became the dominant one in the Latin churches of the West. Toward the end of the third century, Christianity became a powerful force in Rome, and a law was introduced which severely punished women who deliberately procured abortion.[19] In the East, church fathers in the Greek Orthodox Church, such as Basil of Cappadocia, subjected those who committed abortion to an ecclesiastical penalty involving two years of penance, which was the same penalty given to those who committed murder.[20]

Thomas Aquinas, perhaps the leading Christian philosopher and theologian in the Medieval Ages, opposed abortion, but distinguished between the moral gravity of early abortions and that of late ones. He closely followed Aristotelian embryology. Aquinas has been referred to as "the embarrassing saint" of the Roman Catholic Church for his explanation of fetal development. He strongly believed that reason was the defining essence of what it means to be a human person.[21] Since bodily and sense faculties apparently only developed after the eighth week, reason and free will could not be present earlier. This indicated that no human person existed in the first eight weeks of pregnancy. Aquinas believed that in the course of gestation humans are first plants, later become animals, and finally become

---

15. Grassian, *Moral Reasoning*, 246.

16. Hurry, "Termination of Pregnancy," 20.

17. Cohn-Sherbok, *Dictionary of Judaism and Christianity*, 1; Asthma, "Abortion and the Embarrassing Saint," 30.

18. Davis, *Abortion and the Christian*, 4.

19. Hurry, "Termination of Pregnancy," 20.

20. Davis, *Abortion and the Christian*, 4.

21. Asthma, "Abortion and the Embarrassing Saint," 30.

human persons. The Roman Catholic Church officially adopted Aquinas' position in 1322, and as a result the baptism of any prematurely born fetuses without a definite human shape was forbidden.[22] During the Renaissance, the church even codified Aquinas' findings into laws at the Council of Trent (1545–1563), declaring that an individual would not be committing homicide if he or she aborted a fetus prior to its human ensoulment at eight weeks.[23] Aquinas in his philosophy may have justified abortion before the eighth week without intending to do so.

In 1585, Pope Sixtus V, while targeting the prevalent prostitution in Rome at the time, condemned abortion without any distinction between a "formed" (ensouled) and an "unformed" fetus.[24] However, due to the influence of erroneous scientific reports the Church accepted the preformation theory. The theory stated that the fetus had a complete human body at the moment of conception, and that fetal development was simply a continuous increase in size of organs and body structures. It was assumed that these organs and structure were fully present in microscopic form at conception.[25] Both the Aristotelian view and the preformation theory were sidelined as the Cartesian dualism of Descartes (1596–1650) gained influence:

> According to the Cartesian picture, soul and body are two radically different sorts of substances, capable of existing independently. A human being . . . is a combination of these two radically different and interacting substances. The soul, from this perspective, is an immortal, conscious substance that occupies or animates a body for a period of time. When this animation or ensoulment took place was an open question.[26]

Apparently it was still assumed that the ensoulment took place as prescribed by Aristotle. The abortion either of a male fetus after forty days or of a female one after eighty days was considered a mortal sin, which justified eternal torment in hell. In 1869 Pope Pius IX issued a decree declaring that human life effectively began at conception.[27]

By the middle of the eighteenth century when new embryological knowledge became available, and the process of cell division became

22. Grassian, *Moral Reasoning*, 446.
23. Asthma, "Abortion and the Embarrassing Saint," 31.
24. Davis, *Abortion and the Christian*, 5.
25. Grassian, *Moral Reasoning*, 246.
26. Ibid.
27. Ibid., 247.

understandable, the Roman Catholic Church had abandoned the teachings of both Aristotle and Aquinas. The church firmly believed in conception as the time of ensoulment.[28] The firmness of the Roman Catholic Church's stand was evident in 1945 when some Catholic nuns were raped by Russian soldiers in the latter's invasion of Germany. Some of the nuns fell pregnant but were not allowed abortion to avoid the consequences of their embarrassing misfortune.[29]

At present the Roman Catholic Church's Canon 1398 states that persons party to an abortion are automatically excommunicated. Although Martin Luther did not directly address the issue of abortion, his teachings on the original sin and the origins of the human soul had the effect of personalizing the unborn child.[30] John Calvin also viewed the unborn as fully human, in agreement with the early church fathers, Tertullian and Athenagoras. In his commentary on Exodus 21:22, which deals with an accidentally induced premature birth or miscarriage, Calvin wrote:

> This passage at first sight is ambiguous, for if the word death only applies to the pregnant woman, it would not be a capital crime to put an end to the fetus, which would be a great absurdity; for the fetus, though enclosed in the womb of its mother, is already a human being, and it is almost a monstrous crime to rob it of the life which it has not yet begun to enjoy. If it seems more horrible to kill a man in his own house than in a field, because a man's house is his place of most secure refuge, it ought surely to be more atrocious to destroy a fetus in the womb before it has come to light.[31]

In 1920 the Soviet Union became the first country in the world to legalize abortion. In the United Kingdom, the 1929 Infant Life Preservation Act made the killing of a child capable of being born alive an offence.[32] But on 17 February 1936 the British Abortion Law Reform Association was formed to campaign for the legalization of abortion. On 27 April 1968 the Abortion Act effectively legalized the termination of pregnancy for a variety of medical reasons.[33] In the United States, abortion remained largely illegal until 22 January 1973 when the Supreme Court, in the famous *Roe*

28. Davis, *Abortion and the Christian*, 5.
29. Lammers and Verhey, *On Moral Medicine*, 399.
30. Davis, *Abortion and the Christian*, 5.
31. Ibid.; Davis and Denney, *Time for Compassion*, 56.
32. Hurry, "Termination of Pregnancy," 20.
33. Ibid., 21.

v. Wade case, took the controversial step of extending the woman's right to privacy to include the right to get an abortion.[34]

In his encyclical *Humanae Vitae* of 25 July 1968, Pope Paul VI declared:

> The direct interruption of the generative process already begun, and above all directly willed and procured abortion, even for therapeutic reasons, is to be absolutely excluded as licit means of regulating birth.[35]

The Roman Catholic Church states in both codes of Canon Law (Eastern and Western) that anyone who procures an abortion or cooperates in performing an abortion has committed a grave sin needing official forgiveness from the Church.[36] The Vatican Council II also states that human life must be safeguarded with the utmost care from the moment of conception, saying, "Abortion and infanticide are abominable crimes." This is the first statement ever made by a general council of the Church on abortion. Its judgment represents a commitment by the Catholic Bishops of the entire world to care for the developing fetus.[37] Pope John Paul II in his encyclical *Evangelium Vitae* [The Gospel of Life] of 25 March 1995 also defends the sacredness of human life:

> Procured abortion is the deliberate and direct killing, by whatever means it is carried out, of his or her existence, extending from conception to birth. . . . No reason, however serious and tragic, can ever justify the deliberate killing of an innocent human being.[38]

The Roman Catholic Church consistently teaches its members against abortion as an evil against the human race. This is seen by some people who do not subscribe to the faith as a hard-line stand against the reproductive

---

34. Arthur, *Morality and Moral Controversies*, 183. The *Roe v. Wade* case began in August 1969 when Norma McCorvey discovered that she was pregnant. She was too poor to travel from Texas where she lived to California, the nearest state where abortion was legal. A friend of hers introduced her to two recent law school graduates, Sarah Weddington and Linda Coffee, and the three decided to challenge the constitutionality of the law forbidding abortion in Texas. Norma McCorvey never got her abortion, nor did she see her baby again after leaving the hospital. For purposes of the lawsuit she made against Henry Wade, the then district attorney for Dallas Country in Texas, she used a pseudonym, Jane Roe, hoping to remain anonymous. Four years later, on 22 January 1973, the Supreme Court made a decision, which effectively legalized abortion in America.

35. ADS 9–10, no. 501, 3.

36. Ibid.

37. Ibid.

38. Pope John Paul II, *Evangelium Vitae*.

Historical, Biblical and Theological–Ethical Perspectives

rights of women. However, as can be verified from the preceding recollection of the history, the current stand of the church has its derivations from history.

In this historical review section it is clear that concern over the problem of termination of pregnancy was expressed only from the perspectives of either the morality of the act of abortion or the personal status of the unborn. No church father or historical personality seems to have brought up the perspective of human dignity of either the woman or the fetus. This is a gap that needs to be filled through research that may develop a link between the ethical challenge of termination of pregnancy and the quest for human dignity.

BIBLICAL PERSPECTIVES ON THE UNBORN

While the preceding historical review provides us with an understanding on the development of Christianity's traditional opposition to abortion, it is necessary to examine a theological perception based on teachings found in various portions of Scripture. For, although the Bible does not address the problem of abortion as such, it is explicit on what God says about the unborn. The Bible, therefore, enables the Christian ethicist to formulate a theological ethic, which can guide Christians on the problem of abortion. As R. T. H. Dolamo has stated, the abortion issue is not only for experts such as physicians, philosophers and ethicists, but also for the ordinary citizens.[39] As Christians it should be possible to effectively use our biblical knowledge of the unborn to make a meaningful contribution in the ongoing discussion on abortion. Dolamo explains:

> The fact that there is no direct biblical witness on abortion does not necessarily mean that we as Christians cannot arrive theologically at an informed position on abortion. Through its narratives, themes, arguments, claims and convictions, the Bible bears witness to the kind of ethical perspectives on moral life we can glean from it.[40]

Scripture places a high value in conception and refers to it forty times as the start of new life in the womb of the mother. In the Genesis narratives alone, the phrase "conceived and bore" is repeated eleven times. It is

---

39. Dolamo, "Theological Perspective on Abortion," 1.
40. Ibid., 4.

evident that God opens the womb and gives life at conception. In Exodus 23:25–26, God charged the Israelites: "Worship the LORD your God and His blessing will be on your food and water. I will take away sickness from among you, and none will miscarry or be barren in your land. I will give you a full life span." A similar promise is found in Deuteronomy 7:13–14:

> He will love you and bless you and increase your numbers. He will bless the fruit of your womb, the crops of your land—your grain, new wine and oil—the calves of your herds and the lambs of your flocks in the land that he swore to your forefathers to give you. You will be blessed more than any other people; none of your men or women will be childless, nor any of your livestock without young.

In the context of conception being a blessing, God intervened in the lives of barren and frustrated women like Sarah, Rebekah, Rachel, Ruth and Hannah, and enabled them to conceive.

Throughout the entire Bible there appears no suggestion anywhere that abortion is an option for pregnant women. In fact abortion is not even mentioned, possibly because the idea is foreign to biblical culture. Instead, the Bible presents the fruitful wife as one who enjoys God's favor, and children in the home as blessings from God. For instance, Psalm 127:3–5a declares:

> Sons are a heritage from the LORD, children a reward from Him.
> Like arrows in the hands of a warrior are sons born in one's youth.
> Blessed is the man whose quiver is full of them.

In the same theme Psalm 128:1–3 continues:

> Blessed are all who fear the LORD, who walk in His ways.
>   You will eat the fruit of your labor;
>   blessings and prosperity will be yours.
>   Your wife will be like a fruitful vine within your house;
>   your sons will be like olive shoots around your table.

There are, indeed, a few passages in the Bible using personal language to describe the unborn from the moment of conception. Genesis 4:1 describes Cain's conception and birth: "Adam lay with his wife Eve and she became pregnant and gave birth to Cain." Psalm 51:5 states: "Surely I was sinful at birth, sinful from the time my mother conceived me." A number of passages support the view that God knows the unborn in a personal way. Psalm 139:13–16 provides details:

> For you created my inmost being; you knit me together in my mother's womb. I praise you because I am fearfully and wonderfully made. . . . My frame was not hidden from you when I was made in the secret place. When I was woven together in the depths of the earth, your eyes saw my unformed body. All the days ordained for me were written in your book before one of them came to be.

Isaiah 49:1 simply states, "Before I was born the LORD called me; from my birth he has made mention of my name." The same is true in Jeremiah 1:5: "Before I formed you in the womb I knew you; before you were born I set you apart; I appointed you as a prophet to the nations." Such passages clearly indicate that God's special dealings with human beings can long precede their own awareness of a personal relationship with him. Long before society gets used to treating the fetus as a person, God already deals with it in an intensely personal way.

The principal Christian belief that the fetus is made in the image of God is derived from Genesis 5:3, which reads: "When Adam had lived one hundred and thirty years, he had a son in his own likeness, in his own image, and he named him Seth." Fowler suggests that the Hebrew word *yalad*, which is often translated "begot," should be more accurately translated "caused to bring forth," the cause being sexual intercourse and the resulting conception.[41] Assuming that this translation is accurate, although Adam and Eve were the only ones created in God's image, Seth and other descendants of Adam and Eve received the image of God through procreation. It also confirms that Seth's essential human nature was already present at conception. If the image of God pertains to a human being's moral nature, then it becomes extremely hard to argue theologically that one who is not a person can have moral attributes.

There are also a few portions of the Bible, which describe certain personality traits attributed to the fetus *in utero*. Genesis 24:22 reports that Esau and Jacob "jolted each other" while in Rebekah's womb prior to birth. Luke 1:41 describes John the Baptist as having been "filled with the Holy Spirit" while still in Elizabeth's womb. Upon the arrival of Mary with Jesus in her womb, John leaped for joy in the womb. In the same context the unborn are referred to in the same way as young children and infants. The Greek term *brephos* is used in Luke 1:41, 44 to refer to the unborn John as a "baby," while in Luke 2:12, 16 the same word is used to refer to the infant

---

41. Fowler, *Abortion*, 140.

Jesus after birth. These Bible passages seem to teach that there is no inherent difference in status between an unborn fetus and an infant.

Some scholars argue that the Bible passages that mention God's relationship with certain individuals before conception are not relevant to the question of abortion. Francis J. Beckwith responds that God's eternal personality enables him to know all things simultaneously, including knowing each person before conception. Beckwith states that when God speaks of knowing a person prior to conception "he is not making an ontological claim (a being claim), but an epistemological claim (a knowledge claim)."[42] The point is that these references provide support to the thesis that the unborn are persons in God's perspective. Life in the womb is clearly seen as a special stage in the fulfillment of God's plan for an individual. Paul, in Galatians 1:15, says that God had set him apart while still in his mother's womb. As Fowler puts it,

> God's personal involvement with the unborn provides the foundation for their personal worth. If we are persons because God has related to us in a personal way, then the unborn are also persons since God's care for them obviously begins in the womb.[43]

While conception and birth are viewed in the Bible as wonderful blessings from God, miscarriages and murders of the unborn—as pregnant women get ripped open—are viewed as a dreadful curse. In 2 Kings 8:12, Hazel, future king of Aram, asked Elisha why he wept for him. Elisha replied saying, "Because I know the harm you will do to the Israelites. . . . You will set fire to their fortified places, kill their young men with the sword, dash their little children to the ground, and rip open their pregnant women." In Amos 1:13 a prophecy was made against Ammon because they ripped open the pregnant women of Gilead, a cruel act that killed both mother and child. In Hosea's prophecy, due to Israel's sins God would close the nation's wombs. In Hosea 9:14, 16; 13:16, the prophet laments:

> Give them, O LORD—what will you give them?
> Give them wombs that miscarry and breasts that are dry . . .
> Ephraim is blighted, their root is withered, they yield no fruit.
> Even if they bear children, I will slay their cherished offspring . . .
> The people of Samaria must bear their guilt,
>   because they have rebelled against their God.
> They will fall by the sword;

42. Beckwith, "Brave New Bible," 492.
43. Fowler, *Abortion*, 144.

> Their little ones will be dashed to the ground,
> their pregnant women ripped open.

It is repeatedly made clear that miscarriages and the ripping open of pregnant women is the ultimate form of punishment for sin and a sign of a severe curse. It helps explain why abortion was so alien to the Hebrew worldview in which there was no place for the destruction of life in the womb. The implication for the Christian is that abortion deliberately brings on one's own family the fate which in Scripture is the symbol of divine curse.[44] From a Christian theological perspective, knowing God's role in conception, abortion cannot be a legitimate option because it denies the holiness of conception and the divine opening of the womb. Allan R. Bevere reminds us:

> The biblical view is clearly one of life as a gift. Life comes to us from a gracious God who does not owe us anything but gives life to us simply because God wills to do so. . . . To acknowledge the giftedness of life is to continue to acknowledge, unlike those who want to argue for one's personal autonomy over one's body, that our continued existence, and the continued existence of the world is in God's hands, not ours. To accept the gift of life is to accept God's sovereignty.[45]

The biblical passage most frequently referred to by theological writers on abortion is found in Exodus 21:22–25. Abortion advocates quote it to show that the fetus is not a person, while those against abortion use it to propose that the fetus is fully human. Simply stated, the passage can be referred to as a controversial one, which deserves a close exegetical scrutiny presently beyond the scope of this thesis. However, an attempt is herein made to outline clearly and simply the two opposite perspectives. The passage under study reads as follows in the New American Standard Bible:

> And if men struggle with each other and strike a woman with child so that she has a miscarriage, yet there is no further injury, he shall surely be fined as the woman's husband may demand of him; and he shall pay as the judges decide. But if there is any further injury, then you shall appoint as a penalty life for life, eye for eye, tooth for tooth, hand for hand, foot for foot, burn for burn, wound for wound, bruise for bruise.

---

44. Ibid., 146.
45. Bevere, "Abortion," 51.

In this translation the child is viewed as having died of a miscarriage and the reference to "no further injury" refers only to the woman. The penalty is not very serious; only a fine determined perhaps by the age of the fetus or consideration of the loss of a son of daughter.[46] Verses 23–25 thereafter refer to possible harm incurred by the woman in addition to the miscarriage. Since the punishment for the killing of a fetus (a fine) is less than the punishment for killing the mother (death), the fetus is thought not to be a human being, and the passage is thought not to condemn abortion. With this interpretation a pregnant woman's serious concerns—such as trauma from rape or incest, the knowledge of a severely imperiled fetus, the mother's mental or physical well-being, education, or career opportunities—have to take priority over the life of the unborn and justify abortion.

An opposite interpretation may be arrived at after a careful exposition of the historical, cultural and grammatical contexts of the passage. The New International Version gives a rendering of Exodus 21:22–25 as follows:

> If men who are fighting hit a pregnant woman and she gives birth prematurely but there is no serious injury, the offender must be fined whatever the woman's husband demands and the court allows. But if there is serious injury, you are to take life for life, eye for eye, tooth for tooth, hand for hand, foot for foot, burn for burn, wound for wound, bruise for bruise.

Both Fowler and Sprinkle hold to the opinion that premature birth rather than miscarriage is involved in the first half of this passage where there is no serious injury. The two writers have provided a thorough examination, with Sprinkle getting deep into linguistic and exegetical details. In this view the baby is born prematurely, but does not die. Since no serious harm occurs to both mother and child, the fine is proper. The serious injury in verse 23 can refer to either the mother or the child, or both.[47] Fowler gives a reason for preferring the second interpretation:

> The literal translation of verse 22 is "so that the child departs." This cannot refer to a miscarriage. The word normally used for miscarriage in Hebrew is *shakol* and is used in Exodus 23:26. The verb here used is *yatza*, meaning "to go or come forth." It is used elsewhere in Scripture to describe normal births and never refers to a miscarriage.[48]

---

46. Fowler, *Abortion*, 147.
47. Ibid., 148; Sprinkle, "Interpretation of Exodus 21:22–25," 233.
48. Fowler, *Abortion*, 148.

Fowler further argues that there are Hebrew words for fetus *(golem)* or for the death of an unborn child *(nefel)*, usually translated "one untimely born." These words are not found in the passage in Exodus 21:22–25.

Fuller disputes this technical language argument, saying that the word *yatza* used in Exodus 21:22 specified normal births in Job 1:21 and Jeremiah 1:5. He observes, however, that in Numbers 12:12 it referred to a miscarriage, or perhaps a stillbirth. From his perspective, there are no passages in the Hebrew Bible where *yatza* clearly refers to a premature birth.[49] Fuller appeals to the interpretational history of Exodus 21:22:

> The miscarriage interpretation, despite its general language that could have misled later interpreters, held unanimous consent from the LXX (or *the Septuagint*) to Martin Luther some 1800 years. John Calvin was the first to suggest the premature birth view. He was later followed by nineteenth century German scholars such as Keil, Greiger and Dillman.[50]

He concludes that the miscarriage view has the most impressive interpretational history and the securest exegetical foundations.

Despite his vehement onslaught on the premature birth interpretation, Fuller uses both the broader legal context of the ancient Near East and the entire covenant code in Exodus 20:22—23:33 to defend the personhood of the fetus. According to Fuller, the ancient Sumerian and Hittite laws assessed fines for the loss of the fetus without making any reference to the health of the mother. The Sumerian laws determined the fine according to the assailant's intent, whether he struck the pregnant woman accidentally or deliberately. The Hittite laws determined the fine according to fetal development. The ancient Code of Hammurabi, however, contemplated the loss of both the fetus and mother, supplying a closer parallel to the Exodus passage.[51] Fowler's point is that, although the broader ancient Near Eastern legal tradition differentiated legal status by class, sex and age, these did not imply differences in personhood. One person could be fined for a specific crime and another person executed for committing the same crime, without suggesting differences in personhood between the two who committed the crime. They simply differed in legal or social status. Fowler ends by stating that the ancient Near Eastern legal tradition disproves the argument that differences in punishments imply differences in personhood. Apparently,

49. Ibid., 182.
50. Ibid.
51. Fuller, "Exodus 21:22–23," 171.

the Exodus covenant code agrees to this by showing various categories in legal status.

Whether the interpretation is that of a "miscarriage" or that of a "premature birth" appears to be a debatable point, which needs further historical and grammatical research. However, the view proposed in this thesis is that the passage does not in any way indicate differences in personhood. The historical ancient Near Eastern legal context, as well as grammar, supports this view, which presently appears to favor the premature birth position.

In the conception of Jesus, the angel Gabriel told Mary that she would have a child, the beginning of whose life was to be marked by the conception by the Holy Spirit. It may be observed that Jesus' participation in humanity "began where every human life begins—conception."[52] Fowler further comments that this observation is crucial, for it tells us that in God's sight, human life at every stage of development is the object of God's redeeming love. In this respect, Jesus' conception and life in the womb of Mary provides a new and profound status of human dignity for all unborn children.

In this biblical review section discussions point out that God holds highly the dignity and sacredness of human life. The act of pregnancy termination is itself not directly a biblical matter of concern. Instead the status of the unborn is. In the exegetical discussions that follow the various passages, none seems to have clearly focused on the perspective of human dignity of either the woman or the fetus. Again, like the historical review previously, this is a gap that needs to be filled through research that may develop a link between the ethical challenge of termination of pregnancy and the quest for human dignity from a biblical perspective.

THEOLOGICAL-ETHICAL PERSPECTIVES ON TERMINATION OF PREGNANCY

Ethicists writing on the subject of abortion generally seem to fall into either of two categories, namely, pro-choice and pro-life. The two categories accommodate physicians, lawyers, theologians, church ministers and other people interested in ethics. In between the two are writers who would favor abortion in certain circumstances for certain reasons, and would oppose it at times for other reasons.

---

52. Fowler, *Abortion*, 154.

Historical, Biblical and Theological–Ethical Perspectives

Arguments For Termination of Pregnancy

Among the strongest proponents of abortion is Joseph Fletcher who discusses the problem of abortion in relation to issues in genetics and medicine, such as artificial insemination, sperm banking and cloning. Fletcher observes that changing attitudes toward human sexuality and the development of modern contraceptive devices have largely separated sexual activity from procreation. He explains:

> Technology, whether of the "hard" physical kind or the "soft" biological kind, is man's creation and man's hallmark.... Lovemaking and baby making have been divorced. Sex is free from the contingencies and complications of reproduction, and sexual practice can now proceed on its own merits as an independent value in life. ... Make love, not people. This is the rock-bottom fact of the new age and the new morality.[53]

Fletcher, who is on the forefront in advocating for situation ethics, apparently believes that, although moral principles may provide useful guidelines for ethical reflection, they should not be understood to be absolutely binding in every circumstance. For instance, he argues that under certain circumstances it may be legitimate and morally right to violate widely held moral values, such as rules prohibiting adultery and the taking of human life, if a greater personal good would result.[54] With regard to the status of the human fetus, Fletcher proposes that humans without some minimum of intelligence or mental capacity—indicated by a minimum score of twenty on the Binet scale of Intelligence Quotient (IQ)—are not persons, no matter how spontaneous their living processes are. Since the fetus cannot meet the test, Fletcher holds that the unborn become persons at birth, when the umbilical cord is cut and the lungs begin to function.[55] He reasons that whenever the cost-benefit calculation indicates that abortion would be in the woman's best interests it becomes justifiable at any stage of pregnancy. He argues:

> The ethical principle is that pregnancy when wanted is a healthy process; pregnancy when not wanted is a disease—in fact a venereal

---

53. Fletcher, *Ethics of Genetic Control*, 15.
54. Ibid., 16.
55. Ibid., 137.

decease. The truly ethical question is not whether we can justify abortion but whether we can justify compulsory pregnancy.[56]

In this view, abortion must be granted to any pregnant woman who wishes to have it for any reason at any time.

One of the strongest defenses of abortion in philosophical writings is in the article "A Defense of Abortion," by Judith Jarvis Thomson. The essay avoids discussing the status of the fetus, which is regarded by other writers as the central problem in the abortion debate. Thomson defends the right to get an abortion, even if it is to be assumed that the fetus has the same moral status as a child. She disputes the assumption that the morality of abortion depends on when the developing human is considered alive or becomes a person.[57] Her argument is founded in the theory that a woman has the right to refuse the use of her body to a dependent fetus. In this theory, a fetus does not have a right to the use of the mother's body in certain circumstances and its mother has no obligation to afford it that use.[58] In Thomson's view such circumstances should include where the mother's life is at stake, where she has been raped, and where she has voluntarily engaged in sexual intercourse but has taken reasonable precautions to avoid pregnancy. She concludes that, to make it a woman's obligation to accept these "inconveniences" when she is not responsible for her pregnant condition is to force her to be a "Good Samaritan," which the law does not force other people to become.[59]

Thomson uses an interesting analogy of a famous violinist who requires the use of another person's kidneys for nine months to extract poisons from his bloodstream. She goes on to argue that a mother's right to her own body allows her to "unplug" from a fetus even if the fetus is assumed to be a person. She explains that if two sexual partners have taken all reasonable precautions against having a child, they cannot be responsible for any conceived fetus just because they are related to it biologically. Thomson's argument is based on the principle of justice insofar as it applies to the mother. The mother's right to be free from any perceived form of aggression seems to always take precedence over the right of the fetus to be alive. In this principle, the fetus deserves to be removed for "plugging itself" in the mother's womb when it is not welcome to do so, because that act is

56. Ibid., 142.
57. Arthur, *Morality and Moral Controversies*, 188.
58. Grassian, *Moral Reasoning*, 256.
59. Arthur, *Morality and Moral Controversies*, 189.

unjust to the mother. Therefore, the mother has no moral obligation to afford the fetus the use of her body, and would not be acting unjustly if she refused that use. What Thomson does not make reference to is the question of whether it is always just to kill beings that are not tolerated.

In the understanding of Grassian, Thomson's description and moral appraisal using the violinist analogy is Kantian in style. It is not unjust to refuse to afford the use of one's body in the situation because it is not a violation of one's perfect duty. It is only a refusal to provide benevolent assistance to someone to whom one has no special obligation. In the Kantian view, laws should function to assure justice and not to provide for benevolence.[60] Similarly, laws on termination of pregnancy should not force women to become "Good Samaritans" or even "Minimally Decent Samaritans"—when the sacrifice is small. Forcing a woman to carry a pregnancy to term would seek to make her a "Splendid Samaritan" and not merely a "Good Samaritan".[61] However, it is not clear what would count as reasonable precaution to avoid pregnancy. Besides, it would be quite unrealistic to seek to obtain adequate verification that such precautions were taken. Consequently it would be difficult to formulate workable laws distinguishing justifiable from unjustifiable abortions. It appears that voluntary indulgence in sexual intercourse confers some degree of responsibility on the woman and the responsible man.

For some ethicists who hold strongly to the consequentialist view, taking the life of a person, whether by abortion or otherwise, is not always seriously wrong. As Earl Conee points out, the killing of any being, however morally valuable that being is in itself, may happen "to cause enough good or prevent enough harm to have a consequentialist justification."[62] If the abortionist could forecast the greatest good as the health and happiness of the woman, or the possible prevention of harm for her, the killing of the fetus—even if it is agreed to be human—would be justifiable. For Hugo Tristram Engelhardt Jr., religious belief seems to play a significant role. He proposes that, while a Southern Baptist may regard those who terminate pregnancies as those whose values are deformed, an atheist director of an abortion clinic may see no moral evil in abortion. He continues to say that the director may see such choices as paradigmatic presentations of a proper freedom of women to control their own bodies, thus regarding such

---

60. Grassian, *Moral Reasoning*, 257.

61. Arthur, *Morality and Moral Controversies*, 190.

62. Conee, "Metaphysics and the Morality of Abortion," 629.

choices as not just to be secularly protected but as, in any way, praiseworthy.⁶³ Engelhardt denounces the woman who, on religious grounds, refuses abortion after rape.⁶⁴ In his view, such a woman should not be regarded as a brave witness to exemplary moral convictions, but as a woman exploited by a false and patriarchal understanding of values. In secular moral terms, according to Engelhardt, the sperm, ova, zygote, and fetus are extensions and the fruit of one's own body. He says:

> They are one's own to dispose of until they take possession of themselves as conscious entities, until one gives them a special standing in a community, until one transfers one's rights in them to another, or until they become persons. The sense of right here draws attention to the lack of other's authority to impose their will on such private choices.⁶⁵

It appears that, although he begins by highlighting the pivotal role of religious faith in judging the wrongness or rightness of an abortion, Engelhardt concludes that the religious choice against abortion is a result of naivety. His strongest argument seems to be that the fetus is not yet a person and, as such, has no rights. This premise would fall apart if it can be clearly proved, both biologically and philosophically, that the fetus is a person.

The concept of a person has received a lengthy treatment from Jane English who enumerates biological, psychological, rational, social and legal factors which would constitute a person, and which a fetus would need to attain in order to qualify.⁶⁶ The biological factors include descent from humans, having a certain genetic make-up, having a head, hands, arms, eyes, being capable of movement, breathing, eating and sleeping. The psychological factors include the ability to work in groups and respond to peer pressure, the ability to recognize and consider as valuable the interests of others, the ability to sympathies, encourage, love, the ability to evoke from others the response of sympathy, encouragement, love, and the ability to work with others for mutual advantage. Legal factors include being subject to the law and protected by it, having the ability to sue and enter contracts, being counted in the census, having a name and citizenship, and the ability to own property and inherit. Although a person may not meet all the conditions of personhood, he or she needs to meet most of them. Since a fetus

---

63. Engelhardt, *Foundations of Bioethics*, 44.
64. Ibid., 80.
65. Ibid., 256.
66. English, "Abortion and the Concept of a Person," 217.

does not meet most of them, except for the biological ones, he or she may not qualify for personhood, despite having human features. English argues that there is no well-defined line dividing persons from nonpersons.[67] For her, both the conservative and the liberal positions are too extreme, and some abortions are morally justifiable while others are not. She proposes that abortion is justifiable early in pregnancy to avoid modest harms and seldom justifiable in late pregnancy except to avoid significant injury or death. Instead of relying on rights, English urges us to rely on our obligations to others.

Similar arguments are advanced by Warren, who insists that a fetus is not a person, and should not be given full moral rights. She asserts:

> We need not attempt a detailed consideration of the moral rights of organisms which are not developed enough, intelligent enough, etc., to be considered people, but which resemble people in some respects . . . a fetus, even a fully developed one, is considerably less personlike than is the average mature mammal, indeed the average fish.[68]

For Warren it would be a fallacy to conclude that a merely potential person has a right to life by virtue of that potential. In her thought, the rights of a woman far outweigh whatever right to life a fetus may have. It would, for instance, be permissible to let an American woman obtain an abortion to avoid having to postpone a trip to Europe. Such an act, in Warren's view, would not be immoral, and ought to be permitted. She further insists:

> Neither a fetus' resemblance to a person nor its potential for becoming a person provides any basis whatsoever for the claim that it has any significant right to life. Consequently, a woman's right to protect her health, happiness, freedom, and even her life, by terminating an unwanted pregnancy will always override whatever right to life it may be appropriate to ascribe to a fetus, even a fully developed one.[69]

Since the fetus's right to become a person does not provide any basis for ascribing to it any significant right to life, no legislation against abortion can be justified on the grounds of protecting the rights of the fetus. Professor Solomon R. Benatar of the University of Cape Town's Department of

---

67. Ibid., 216.
68. Warren, "On the Moral and Legal Status of Abortion," 25.
69. Ibid.

Medicine observes that, although a fetus is unquestionably a living organism and a member of the human species, it does not possess any characteristics of personhood in the same way adults do. He proposes that the fetus's acquisition of rights is more gradual and that obligations to preserve it increase as pregnancy progresses.[70]

There is also the theory that an entity cannot have a right to life unless it is capable of having an interest in its own continued existence. Michael Tooley, a leading proponent of this theory, suggests that an entity is not capable of having an interest in its own continued existence unless it possesses, at some time, the concept of a continuing self, as a continuing subject of experiences and other mental states.[71] Tooley concludes, "The fact that an entity will, if not destroyed, come to have properties that would give it a right to life, does not in itself make it seriously wrong to destroy it." He introduces the concept of a "quasi-person" which he defines as "a being that possesses the properties for being a person at a very low degree."[72] Such a being has some degree of a right to life. Since, according to Tooley, human beings become quasi-persons at the age of three months after birth, infanticide is morally permissible on newborns.[73]

In 1970, Howard Moody was the pastor of Judson Memorial Church in New York City, a director of the New York Civil Liberties Union, and a leader in the founding of the Clergy Consultation Service on Abortion, which referred thousands of women for safe abortions. Moody says that the actual process of working with women compelled him, and others, to move beyond strictly theoretical hang-ups:

> In this process we always had to consider the moral question of whether it is justifiable to force the unwanted upon the unwilling. In our anxiety to honor the theory of the sanctity of life in general, we have always played fast and loose with particular women's lives and forced them by legal fiat to bear children that they never intended to conceive. To use a woman's body, against her free will and choice, as a receptacle for unwanted pregnancy has got to be seen as a kind of legalized rape that must be as morally repugnant as feticide to those perpetrating it.[74]

70. Benatar, "Abortion," 470.
71. Olen and Barry, *Applying Ethics*, 176.
72. Grassian, *Moral Reasoning*, 254.
73. Ibid.
74. Moody, "Abortion," 338.

Moody argues that the unwanted and consequently frequently unloved child often has a malformed spirit and a mutilated psyche. He claims that the child abuse syndrome is directly related to resented and unloved children. He, then, suggests that the formulation of ethical conclusions and action be based on the context of actual contact with the persons involved, their need and predicament.[75] For Moody, theological reflection or moral principles are practically irrelevant.

This position is supported by Welekeza P. Jakuja, who points out that, within African communities, in a case of conception by rape, the child may not be accepted by the girl's or woman's family and by the society at large.[76] Besides, such pregnancy will be a constant reminder of the violent and humiliating act of rape. Jakuja further points out that an unwanted pregnancy may threaten the physical, psychological or mental health of the mother, who may already be overburdened by her existing children or by family problems.[77] Such cases justify abortion, in Jakuja's opinion. Although he admits that the taking of human life is prohibited in Scriptures, he insists that it is sanctioned in extenuating circumstances. However, he does not explain those extenuating circumstances in which the taking of innocent human life would be permissible. It is also unclear as to whether abortion can really solve a health problem or worsen it, especially if it is psychological.

One theological issue worth examining is that brought up by Richard Schoening concerning human post-mortem existence in eternity as it relates to abortion. The Christian faith teaches that there will be incomparable joy in heaven for the saved that meet certain criteria. In contrast, there will be acute suffering in hell for the condemned. The receipt of eternal salvation and the avoidance of eternal doom are the most significant goals for the Christian. Schoening's argument proposes that, since God would like all people to be saved, it follows that the aborted fetuses are beneficiaries of God's omni-benevolence.[78] The aborted fetuses are presumed innocent and are not held responsible for their being aborted. This is compatible with the doctrine of the Southern Baptists who state that "up to the point of accountability, however, Christ's atonement covers the human race, and all who die before reaching this stage of development are saved."[79] This

---

75. Ibid., 339.
76. Jakuja, "Ethical Implications," 61.
77. Ibid., 71.
78. Schoening, "Abortion, Christianity, and Consistency," 32.
79. Ibid., 33.

interpretation of Christian soteriology followed to its logical end, gives the aborted fetuses an enormous salvific advantage over most other human beings. In Schoening's reasoning, abortion is justified by its end, which is the enabling of the fetus to enjoy eternal life. Although abortion would cause some physical and psychological harm to the parents, such harm would be bearable to parents who would endure in order to guarantee the eternal salvation of their offspring. Schoening finds it awkward that God would punish parents for facilitating the *summum bonum* (the highest good) of their children. He argues:

> If parents would be willing to trade something even more important to them than their own lives, namely, their own chances of salvation, for the eternal happiness of their children, this willingness should strengthen their case for forgiveness from a loving and compassionate God who could not fail to see the selfless quality of such actions.[80]

Schoening's reasoning appears to be faulty because a morally wrong act cannot have positive results. For instance, although we know from the Bible that pregnancy and birth are blessings from God, we cannot use that fact to justify all rape and incest, which may result in a conception. Similarly, the murder of a righteous Christian may mean that the murdered Christian will go to heaven. But the Christian's going to heaven does not justify his murder. In any case, violently sending people to heaven is not a human responsibility; protecting human life is. Abortion cannot be justified merely because it sends fetuses to heaven. Parents do not gain any special favor in God's eyes by aborting to send the fetus to heaven, just as they would not benefit in any way by killing youthful children in order to send them to heaven. Furthermore, God's forgiveness does not morally justify an abortion, just as it does not justify any other moral sin.

The other soteriological issue raised by Schoening concerns the fate of frozen fertilized human eggs. The concern is legitimate because, in clinics carrying out *in vitro* fertilization services, in the most common procedures, eight eggs are harvested from the prospective mother and fertilized at once. Four of the fertilized eggs are used for the procedure while four others are frozen for future use. Most of the frozen fertilized eggs are in a very early stage of undifferentiated development of two to four cells.[81] It is likely that there are tens of thousands of frozen zygotes throughout the

---

80. Ibid.
81. Ibid., 35.

world in which no one has any interest, and the legal question remains unsettled. Schoening blames abortion opponents for not insisting that capable females provide their wombs to bring these zygotes to birth.[82] From an ethical point of view, if the costs involved could somehow be taken care of by the state, it would be worth considering the use of artificial wombs to enable the frozen embryos to grow to maturity and birth. Thereafter, such children could either be available for adoption by childless couples or be under the legal care of trustees appointed by the state. Alternatively, they could be brought up in institutions set up by either the state or the church.

In this section reviewing perspectives of proponents of pregnancy termination, arguments have been advanced to support the morality of the act of abortion, the rights of the woman, or the status of the unborn. No argument seems to have been raised from the perspective of human dignity of either the woman or the fetus. As has already been noted in the previous historical and biblical sections, this is a gap that needs to be filled through research that may develop a link between the ethical challenge of termination of pregnancy and the quest for human dignity in order to resolve the ethical problem of termination of pregnancy.

Arguments Against Termination of Pregnancy

The traditional Roman Catholic position on abortion is based on the principle of double effect, and affirms that a pregnant woman never has a right to directly intend—either as an end or as a means—the death of the fetus she is carrying.[83] The Roman Catholic moralists theorize that, "while it is permissible to remove the cancerous uterus of a pregnant woman, thereby indirectly killing the fetus, one cannot morally perform a craniotomy in which the skull of a fetus in the process of being born is crushed, since this would be a direct abortion."[84] A case in point is one in which a woman's egg is fertilized in one of her fallopian tubes. If it is left on its own to develop, it will rupture the tube and kill both the mother and fetus. In the Roman Catholic theory, it would be permissible to remove her fallopian tube through a surgical operation, thereby causing an indirect abortion, but impermissible to kill the fetus through a Dilation & Curettage (D&C). It would be morally wrong to directly kill a fetus to save a mother's life,

82. Ibid., 36.
83. Grassian, *Moral Reasoning*, 258.
84. Ibid.

even if both will die if nothing is done. Even if the pregnant woman were to become sterile, that would be a morally better choice than to intentionally kill the fetus through a D&C. The underlying concept in the church is that it is better for both innocent people to die as a result of an act of God than for some human being to directly intend the death of one, even if he can save the other in the process.[85]

The passage in Hebrews 7:9–10 states that Levi, who himself received tithes, paid tithes through Abraham, for he was still in the loins of his ancestor when Melchizedek met him. Erickson points out that this passage is evidence of traducianism, the theological view that the entirety of a person's human nature, both material and immaterial—or body and soul—is received from parents.[86] The soul is not, at some later time, such as birth, infused into the body, which was physically generated at conception. This would in turn argue for the humanity of the fetus, since it would be impossible to think of a fetus without a soul or a spiritual nature. Although he concedes that no biblical passage clearly states that the fetus is a human being, he concludes that a conservative approach would be prudent where the possibility exists of destroying human life. Erickson warns:

> If one is hunting and sees a moving object which may be either a deer or another hunter, or if one is driving and sees what may be either a pile of rags or a child lying in the street, one will assume that it is a human. And a conscientious Christian will treat a fetus as human, since it is highly likely that God regards a fetus as a person capable of—at least potentially—that fellowship with God for which man was created.[87]

Ethicists who argue either philosophically or theologically that abortion is morally wrong are usually referred to as pro-life ethicists. Don Marquis describes an anti-abortionist argument as one based on such factors as: that life is present from the moment of conception, or that fetuses look like babies, or that fetuses possess a genetic code that is both necessary and sufficient for being human.[88] A typical pro-choice argument asserts that fetuses are not rational agents or that fetuses are not social beings. Marquis explains that the anti-abortionist defends the moral principle of the wrongness of killing in a broad scope so that even the early fetus will be

---

85. Grassian, *Moral Reasoning*, 259.
86. Erickson, *Concise Dictionary of Christian Theology*, 553.
87. Ibid., 556.
88. Marquis, "Why Abortion Is Immoral," 208.

included.⁸⁹ The problem with broad principles, according to Marquis, is that they embrace too much. The pro-choice argument defends the same moral principle, but in a narrow scope so that fetuses are excluded. The problem with narrow principles is that they embrace too little.

According to Marquis, the solution to the apparent stand-off lies in an understanding of why it is wrong to kill an innocent adult human being. He explains:

> What primarily makes killing wrong is neither its effect on the murderer nor its effect on the victim's friends and relatives, but its effect on the victim. The loss of one's life is one of the greatest losses one can suffer. The loss of one's life deprives one of all the experiences, activities, projects, and enjoyments that would otherwise have constituted one's future.⁹⁰

For Marquis, killing a human being is wrong, primarily because it leads to the loss of one's future. The experiences, activities, projects and enjoyments referred to are considered valuable either for their own sake or as means to some other valuable happenings. In this argument, abortion is wrong because it is presumed that the fetus has a future of value. The problem worth pointing out in this idea is that killing does not appear to be necessarily wrong when it is committed on people who are sick and dying. People who are perceived to be having no potentially enjoyable future are not protected by this theory, and can be easily killed at will. Hence, it does not make it wrong to abort a fetus that has been diagnosed to be severely imperiled with, say, Down's syndrome, or spina bifida.

The approach adopted by Baruch Brody is to look at when human life ends—a topic obviously relevant to euthanasia—and to use the answer to that question as a way of attacking the problem of when life begins. In his opinion there are two options, both of which would justify early abortions. One is brain death, and the other is the revised traditional position, which holds that a functioning heart, respiratory system, or brain is enough condition for life.⁹¹ Brody then presents two considerations usually cited in support of abortion in the case of a pregnancy resulting from rape. The first one is that the woman in question has already suffered immensely from the act of rape, both physically and emotionally. The second is that the fetus in question has no right to be in that woman, since it has been put there as a

---

89. Ibid., 209.
90. Ibid., 212.
91. Brody, "Opposition to Abortion," 195.

result of an act of aggression.[92] But Brody goes further and introduces the idea of justice in opposing abortion even in such pregnancies. He argues that, however unjust the act of rape, the fetus neither committed nor commissioned it.[93] He continues to say,

> The injustice of the act, then, should in no way impinge upon the rights of the fetus, for it is innocent. What remains is the initial misfortune of the mother and the injustice of her having to pass through the pregnancy and, further, to assume responsibility of at least giving the child over for adoption or assuming the burden of its care.[94]

While acknowledging the unfortunate circumstances of a pregnancy through rape, and the injustice involved therein, Brody's plea is that these are not sufficient cause to justify the killing of an innocent human being as a means of mitigation. The fetus has human rights, which are a strong basis for moral opposition to abortion.

This perspective is supported by Fowler who, while acknowledging that rape and incest are horrible experiences, argues that one wrong does not correct another wrong. One act of violence is not solved by another violent act. He continues to emphasize the violent nature of abortion:

> Abortion is a violent act. Its methods are physically violent, the painful effects on the child can be termed none other than violent, and the consequent effect on those participating in the abortion bespeaks violence.... The immediate and long-term effect of abortion on mothers is harmful both physically and psychologically.[95]

Some abortions are based on the fetus's disability. This results from and in turn strengthens beliefs such as: children with disabilities, and by implication adults with disabilities, are a burden to family and society; life with a disability is scarcely worth living; preventing such a birth is an act of kindness; women who bear disabled children have failed. Although raising a child with disabilities is difficult, it is true that raising any child is difficult anyway. However, a child with disabilities can enrich a parent's life. Fowler criticizes the media for often portraying raising a child with disabilities as

---

92. Ibid., 200.
93. Ibid.
94. Ibid.
95. Fowler, *Abortion*, 171.

personal martyrdom, and for promoting a society in which disabled children, disabled people, are viewed as misfortunes.

For some, like Gail Hinich Sutherland, the causal relationship between sexual pleasure and the resultant pregnancy cannot be ignored in the current abortion debate. The point, for the normative Christian view of sexuality, is to strike a balance between sexual pleasure, which is self-centered and unproductive, and duty, which is other oriented and socially constructive. The latter redeems the former. Pregnancy is a manifestation of the relationship between the two.[96] In Sutherland's view, abortion strips the sexual act of all redemptive possibility. The strength of Sutherland's viewpoint is in its attempt to restore the bond between sexual pleasure and human reproductive faculties. While sexual intercourse is not only meant for reproduction, pleasure is not meant to be an end in itself either; human responsibility has to be practiced to enhance human relationships. Abortion seems to promote pleasure as the only goal of sexual intercourse, and seeks to avoid responsibility in human sexuality. Sutherland's view finds support in McQuilkin, who observes:

> The pregnant woman has made a prior choice to have sexual intercourse, a choice which brought another party into her life, a separate individual whose rights now limit her own freedom of choice. Choices often lead to conditions that are physically or morally irreversible. Her choice as to what happens to and in her body should have been made earlier. It is too late to choose for or against motherhood. The pregnant woman is already a mother.[97]

In Tom L. Huffman's thought, a pregnant woman is responsible for the very existence of the threat she now faces if she knowingly and voluntarily engages in procreative sex with a man. It is clear that the fetus has no contributory role at all in placing itself in a position of dependency. He argues that the fetus has as much right to self-defense as has the pregnant mother. He explains:

> If it is proper to consider a woman's right to employ a physician in self-defense against an unwanted fetus, then it is equally proper to consider an interested third-party exercising the fetus' right of self-defense on its behalf against a woman who intends to abort. The fetus is . . . a moral patient who has a right to life but must

---

96. Sutherland, "Abortion and Woman's Nature," 603.
97. McQuilkin, *Introduction to Biblical Ethics*, 323.

rely upon others to protect it against those who would threaten its interests.[98]

The fetus is therein viewed as one with rights worthy of protection, and the role of protecting the fetuses right to life has to be taken up by others on its behalf. This argument effectively answers the self-defense principle usually advanced in support of a woman's right to abort. Thomson's theory of unplugging the fetus in the same manner as one would unplug "the violinist" comes to mind as one that ignores the welfare of the fetus and its right to life, if it may be classified as a person.

Early feminists such as Susan B. Anthony viewed abortion as child murder and believed that it exploited both women and children. Anthony's newspaper, the *Revolution*, (8 July 1961) stated that "when a woman destroys the life of her unborn child it is a sign that by education or circumstances she has been greatly wronged."[99] In a letter to Julie Ward Howe's journal of 16 October 1973, Elizabeth Cady Stanton, another leading feminist said: "When we consider that women are treated as property, it is degrading to women that we should treat our children as property to be disposed of as we wish."[100] In the view of these women, abortion allowed men to abdicate all responsibility for their sexual behavior and to regard women as objects for exploitation. Downs argues against aborting a baby conceived by rape, saying this "perpetuates the same disregard for the right to life as is experienced by the woman whose right over her body and privacy is disregarded by the act of rape."[101]

In the abortion debate, Christian ethicists must take care of arguments that seem to dehumanize and trivialize the death of the fetus as a way to humanize and make important the reproductive rights of women. If a fetus can simply be evicted from the womb because it has not attained full personhood, it appears there is nothing to prevent the killing of other "inconvenient" human lives such as the severely handicapped, the dysfunctional, the senile, and the mentally ill. Society must be encouraged not to regard women's fertility as a burden, but as a gift. Edith Schaeffer gives a graphic description of what abortion does:

---

98. Huffman, "Abortion, Moral Responsibility, and Self Defense," 298.
99. Downs, "Opposing Abortion," 48.
100. Ibid.
101. Ibid., 52.

Historical, Biblical and Theological–Ethical Perspectives

> Aborting life, snuffing out tiny, growing people, murdering boys and girls of all nationalities, burning and destroying perfect little hearts, fingers and toes, brains and ears, vocal cords and wee feet, all just weeks away from being able to be washed, clothed, fed, cuddled, and affected for a lifetime by a warm and loving welcome into the world—what a career![102]

In Schaeffer's view, abortion denies the woman the chance of ever hearing her own child's voice, or seeing the color of her eyes, or nature of her hair; the woman will never know whether her child's mind was mathematical or philosophical. The value of that loss to the woman is too great to justify an abortion. Former US Surgeon General C. Everett Koop has this to say on the stage of pregnancy at which abortion would be permissible:

> I do not know anyone among my medical confreres, no matter how pro-abortion he might be, who would kill a newborn baby the minute after he was born. . . . My question is this: Would you kill this infant a minute before that, or a minute before that, or a minute before that? . . . At what minute can one consider life to be worthless and the next minute consider that same life to be precious?[103]

Koop's question is more pertinent in view of the fact that arguments in support of abortion have a tendency to emphasize a function-based definition of personhood. Function as a basis of deciding on personhood makes one wonder whether a basketball player ceases to be one when singing in the choir. A fetus may not function in the same way adults do, but that fact alone may not remove from the fetus the status of a person.

In this section reviewing perspectives of opponents of pregnancy termination, arguments have been advanced to oppose the morality of the act of abortion, the rights of the fetus over against those of the mother, or the status of the unborn. No argument seems to have been raised from the perspective of human dignity of either the woman or the fetus. The arguments raised strongly defend the rights of the fetus, but falls short of raising any issues of human dignity. As has already been noted in the previous historical and biblical sections, as well as the section reviewing the perspectives of proponents of pregnancy termination, this is a gap that needs to be filled through research. Such research may develop a link between the ethical

---

102. Schaeffer, *Lifelines*, 127.
103. Koop, *Right to Live, the Right to Die*, 27.

challenge of termination of pregnancy and the quest for human dignity in order to resolve the ethical problem of termination of pregnancy.

SUMMARY

The foregoing reviews of the various perspectives on abortion gives insights into two viewpoints, namely, pro-life and pro-choice. Apparently, the strongest pro-choice argument is one that asserts the woman's personal autonomy and control over her own body. Since it is clear from biological knowledge of fetal prenatal development that the unborn entity is not part of the pregnant woman's body, abortion cannot be justified. No one's right to personal autonomy is strong enough to permit the arbitrary execution of others. Thomson's powerful illustration on unplugging the violinist is philosophically sophisticated. Her argument is that even if the unborn fetus has a right to life, a woman must not be forced to use her bodily organs to sustain the fetus's life. However, the main problem with the violinist illustrations is its implication that all moral obligations must be voluntarily accepted in order to be morally enforceable. Not all moral obligations to one's offspring are voluntary. For instance, in child support laws, a father would be required to pay support for his child primarily because of his biological relationship to the child. By the same analogy, the mother's unwillingness to carry a pregnancy to term is not enough moral ground for the removal of the fetus from the womb.

This chapter has provided a review of historical, biblical and theological-ethical perspectives (both supporting and opposing abortion), thereby leading to adequate understanding of the ethical challenge from those perspectives. The evidently missing portion is that the issue of human dignity has not been linked to abortion in any way that may help develop a resolution to the problem. This makes this research necessary, as it seeks to integrate the aspect of human dignity into the ethical challenge of termination of pregnancy in order to develop resolutions for the church's approach.

CHAPTER 3

CAUSES, PROCEDURES AND CONSEQUENCES OF TERMINATION OF PREGNANCY

INTRODUCTION

This chapter seeks to develop an understanding of the problem of termination of pregnancy, through a review of available information on the causes, procedures and consequences of the practice. The two objectives here are to enable the reader to appreciate the magnitude of the problem and to identify the human dignity gaps that have continually left the problem largely unresolved, especially in the Kenyan context.

FACTORS LEADING TO PREGNANCY TERMINATION

Socioeconomic Factors

Many women who have had abortions say they did so because it seemed the only alternative to an unwanted pregnancy. Even if they would have considered other options, they did not receive support from friends, relatives, or counselors. Besides, they did not have the emotional strength to investigate other options on their own. To such women, abortion became the easy solution to their predicament. Sappington regrets that abortion is one of the few instances in which the decisions are made in isolation, adding the remark that the expression "between a woman and her doctor" usually means "between a woman and an abortionist she has never met before."[1] Zimmerman observes that an unmarried pregnant woman may feel worried, angry, guilty, excited, bitter, scared, dazed, uptight, trapped, nervous, resentful, used, ashamed, alone, depressed, caught and overwhelmed.[2] All these factors combine to make her vulnerable.

The social stigma caused by an unexpected pregnancy is another cause for concern, as Michels (1988:18) observes:

> Becoming pregnant, whether a woman is married or unmarried, betrays her active sexuality. If she is unmarried, she feels she has been caught; all of her friends and relatives will know she is sexually active. So if she can terminate the pregnancy before it is obvious, no one will know she was pregnant or even had a sexual relationship.[3]

The prevalence of abortion is enhanced by the social-cultural situations in which women get sexually active and become pregnant. Among the Luo[4] in Kenya, for instance, a girl who conceives before marriage is termed *nyako mochwanyore*, which literally means "a girl who has had an accident." She has made a mistake in her life, which would become a permanent reminder of her looseness. Custom, in earlier times, would demand that such girls be married off to elderly old men. In today's society, however, they find it hard to marry even an old man. Old men are now not willing to marry them because the modern economy cannot allow the practice to continue smoothly. Besides, the influence of Christianity strongly discourages polygamous marriages. If a girl discovers today that she is pregnant, she is likely to seek an abortion as a solution. Other ethnic groups in Kenya, and possibly elsewhere in Africa, have their own equivalent customs. The situation is made worse by the difficulty faced by adolescents trying to obtain contra-

---

1. Sappington, "Abortion," 189.
2. Zimmerman, *Should I Keep My Baby?*, 15.
3. Michels, *Helping Women Recover from Abortion*, 18.
4. The Luo are a Nilotic ethnic group residing mainly along the shores of Lake Victoria and in almost all urban areas, towns and cities of East Africa. The community has a rich cultural heritage that persistently influences the modern intellectual and religious lives of its members. The author ethnically belongs to the Luo community and provides this information as a competent and qualified insider.

ceptives. Culture does not allow unmarried girls to go for family planning. The researcher observes that there is no equivalent customary requirement for boys or men who are responsible for pregnancy out of marriage bonds. As such, the burden of sexual purity lies on girls and women, with men becoming mere spectators in the process. Such a situation is unjust, and calls for a process of change.

In addition to the social stigma that a woman may fear, a husband may want his wife to work outside the home without the distraction of childbearing and child rearing. Moreover, an unmarried man may encourage abortion to avoid marriage or the responsibility of financial support for the child. A teenage boy may also support an abortion in order to avoid having to tell his parents that he is the father of a child. John Stott describes the pathetic and desperate situations in which some pregnant women find themselves:

> Their family is already overcrowded and their budget overstretched. Or the mother is herself the wage earner because she is widowed or divorced, or her husband is sick or unemployed. The situation could also be such that the husband is cruel, perhaps an alcoholic, or even a psychopath. Maybe the woman has contracted rubella, or a serious cardiac condition such that she will die if she carries the baby to term.[5]

One of the underlying causes of abortion is the increasing sexual permissiveness among teenagers, besides the lack of proper sexual education and appropriate counseling. There is also the breakdown of traditional African family values, the weakening of religious moral values, and a growing lack of respect for women.

The Catholic Bishops of Zambia add that poverty is one of the main causes that pressurize women to resort to abortions. Poverty is a factor in situations where men—the kind known as "sugar daddies"—take sexual advantage over poor women, then later shun their responsibility for the resultant pregnancies.[6] Such men pressure the women to destroy the newly conceived fetus. Poor women, after having been exploited by men for sexual favors, may not really have a choice, and are forced into abortion by difficult circumstances in which they find themselves.

The problem of abortion in Kenya is deeply rooted in the socialeconomic conditions in which Kenyans live. The most severe of these is

---

5. Stott, Issues Facing Christians Today, 283.
6. ADS 2/1998, no. 485, 3.

poverty, which currently affects the majority in the population. Poverty creates conditions in which families are unable to afford basic necessities for their children, especially girls. Girls who reach puberty and adolescence face peer pressure to look beautiful and well groomed with modern dresses, lotions, and perfumes. Such girls easily engage in sexual activity with working class men in order to gain access to money for such provisions. Often this leads to unwanted pregnancies among schoolgirls, some of whom may opt for abortion.

Poverty also denies recreational facilities to the slum-dwelling populations, most of whom engage in sex as a form of entertainment. If the type of man responsible is not the kind of father a woman would like for her child, she could opt to abort. Besides, people who live in situations of poverty are not able to easily access contraceptives. Illegal unsafe abortion is the only way they can ensure they do not carry unwanted pregnancy to term.

Since there is a general breakdown of moral values that were held strongly in traditional societies, the youth copy lots of behavioral patterns from the West, which promotes individual freedom and free romance. Traditional values of chastity are viewed as backward, while the media portrays promiscuity as progressive. People who become pregnant in such circumstances see abortion as an easy alternative.

There are teenage boys who are sexually active, but are not yet ready to marry and establish a family. Usually such boys encourage their pregnant partners to seek abortion. Parents have also been known to seek abortion for their pregnant daughters in order to take care of their social, religious or political status. For instance, a church elder may put pressure on the pregnant daughter to abort in order to safeguard his image as a very religious man.

There are a number of abortions resulting from factors other than poverty. There are those who go ahead with abortion following the teaching that the fetus is mere tissue and not really a baby. Or that abortion would cause relief from the problem. The teachings may be from peers, doctors, teachers or parents.

Among schoolgirls, perhaps the most significant factor relating to abortion is the education policy. The policy of expelling pregnant girls from school only drives them into fear. As soon as a girl discovers or suspects she is pregnant she seeks an abortion in order to conceal the facts of sexual activity and pregnancy. She would do this to have the chance of continuing with education. In Kenya, pregnancy is, in effect, an educational crime with very severe consequences on girls.

A study was done in Kenya involving 1,077 women who were admitted and treated for incomplete abortion and its related problems. The study concluded that the main determining factor for the termination of pregnancy among the women appeared to be the fact that it was either unwanted or unplanned, or both, mainly because of inappropriate timing, the type of man responsible, the relationship itself, and the socioeconomic implications of the pregnancy. The study also showed that induced unsafe abortion was more common among young, single women, schoolgirls, and young women in urban settings.[7]

There are a number of factors that lead to the scenario where a woman has to decide for abortion. In Kenya schoolgirls who get pregnant are usually expelled from school. A pregnant schoolgirl who wishes to pursue her education may opt for an abortion in order to continue with school uninterrupted. In cases where contraception was used during intercourse, the woman may suddenly get caught when contraception fails. Since society does not tolerate pregnancy among unmarried young women, she may feel pressured into an abortion. As Henry Okullu recollects, a woman may seek an abortion "if her education or career is in jeopardy, if she lacks money to bring up the child, if she fears losing personal freedom or if she wants to wipe out the stigma of her sexual misconduct."[8]

Medical Factors

The most significant factor is that of a disability diagnosed in a prenatal test. An example of a highly feared disability is Down's syndrome, a genetic abnormality of the twenty-first chromosome, the same chromosome that controls collagen development. The neurons of an unborn infant with Down's syndrome are like those of a normal infant. But after about four months, an excess of hydrogen peroxide in babies with Down's syndrome causes apoptosis (cell death) leading to mental retardation. The condition is commonly known as mongolism. Other problems from which a severely imperiled fetus may suffer include the following: spina bifida, a cleft spine through which the membrane that covers the spinal cord protrudes;

---

7. Lema et al., "Induced Abortion in Kenya," 164.
8. Okullu, *Church and Marriage in East Africa*, 52.

Tay-Sachs disease,[9] a neurological disorder; neural tube defect, a severe defect of the brain and spinal cord; Lesch-Nyhan syndrome, a condition of profound mental retardation and features of brain damage such as stiff limbs, peculiar movements and self mutilation; anencephalus, a state in which an infant is born with most or all their brain missing; and hydrocephalus, an accumulation of fluid in an enlarged head resulting in retardation and convulsions. Although many lives of imperiled infants are saved and lengthened, a number of them remain technology dependent and cannot, in any way, interact with the surroundings. Many remain handicapped for life and have to be on constant medication. In order to avoid such an eventuality, some couples opt for abortion as soon as a prenatal diagnosis confirms the disability of the fetus.

METHODS USED IN PREGNANCY TERMINATION

There exists a reasonably large variety of ways in which abortions are carried out. Beside the universally known medical procedures in the act, there are several crude methods, which include objects, chemicals, and herbs. These are worthy of review in order to aid an appreciation of what termination of pregnancy in Kenya involves.

Crude Methods Used in Pregnancy Termination

The expression "crude methods" is used here to imply methods of abortion that are neither carried out nor approved by qualified medical doctors. In most cases, such methods are used in privacy at home, in the bush, or in the back streets of urban centers. S. Talcott Camp reports the use of sharp objects such as knitting needles, or harsh chemicals such as chlorides, in South Africa.[10] Khama O. Rogo tells of traditional herbal medicine for manual manipulation of internal genitalia to procure abortion among the Maasai and other tribes in Kenya.[11] He also reports of outlets run by ill-trained paramedical staff or totally untrained personnel who, at a low fee, provoke vaginal bleeding and instruct the patient to rush to a public hospital soon

---

9. Smedes, *Mere Morality*, 136. Tay Sachs strikes Jewish children of Eastern European background and kills them painfully after a miserably brief life. This makes it a factor of consideration for termination of pregnancy among Eastern European Jewry.

10. Camp, "Why Have You Been Silent?," 59.

11. Rogo et al., "Induced Abortion," 15.

after in order to have the abortion procedure completed safely. They mainly use rubber catheters or other equipment illegally obtained from hospitals.[12] Other women are self-aborts who induce abortion either by ingesting presumed abortifacients or by introducing foreign bodies up the cervix. A research carried out in Nairobi indicates that the most common abortion tool is the rubber catheter, which is inserted into the vaginal tract and into the womb to detach the fetus from the uterus.[13]

Reports from other parts of Africa indicate a similar magnitude of the use of crude methods in obtaining abortion. Sai documents methods used to induce abortion in Africa to include the insertion of an intra-uterine device (IUD) or plastic cannula and other objects such as sticks and plants into the cervix. Traditional healers, private doctors, or midwives employ these facilities. Many desperate women have resorted to drinking gasoline and other toxic substances in an attempt to induce an abortion.[14] In Burkina Faso, traditional practitioners or the abortion seekers themselves mostly use chemical methods. They also use plant concoctions, which are taken orally.[15] The insertion of potassium permanganate suppositories into the vagina has also been reported. Rogo talks of an imaginative use of concoctions like ordinary writing ink, insertion into the cervix foreign bodies such as bones, wires, knitting needles, sticks, and rubber catheters, and high doses of non-prescription anti-malarial medicines, which can be bought in any shop. He also mentions tea leaves being used in East Africa, and the bark of the avocado tree, ginger, and the leaf of "bigarade" in the Seychelles.[16]

In Madagascar there are popular abortion herbs that have been handed down from one generation to the next. The *nifin'akanga* (comonelina madagascaria) is a plant that provokes quick distension of the pelvis. It is used in a decoction and a small bunch is inserted into the vagina. The *rotra gasy* (eugenia), which can cause sterility, is used in a decoction, like the *tango go* (soothly uncinulata) plant, which is said to procure quick delivery. The leaves and the bark of the avocado tree are also used to form a decoction. While the leaves have hypotensive power, the bark causes heavy bleeding while having a tonic value. Aloe seeds, found in the South of Madagascar

---

12. Ibid., 18.
13. Sjostrand et al., "Socio-Economic Client Characteristics," 325.
14. Sai, "Overview of Unsafe Abortion," 2, 3.
15. Passé, "State of Unsafe Abortion in Burkina Faso," 66.
16. Rogo et al., "Induced Abortion," 18.

are used, both as contraceptives and abortifacients. Four seeds are swallowed before sexual intercourse while another four are to be swallowed during the next three days. Other crude formulas in Madagascar include taking a fatal dose of anti-malarial tablets, abdominal traumatism (blows, massage, etc.), and vaginal douche with bleach, puncturing the fertilized egg with a knitting needle or other sharp objects.[17]

All the various tools and methods described above constitute what is known in medical circles as unsafe abortion. It leads to severe physical consequences, such as severe bleeding, sometimes resulting in death. In countries where abortion is illegal, such unsafe procedures are the only alternatives to women. Even in countries where abortion is legal, the monetary constraints involved may lead low-income earners to resort to these methods. Most of the abortions induced in this way are completed in public hospitals. The cases that do not end up in hospitals either die in pain, or live with severe damage in their reproductive systems.

Medical Procedures in Pregnancy Termination

There are four common methods of pregnancy termination described by a number of writers who have written widely on the problem of abortion. The four methods are dilation and curettage (D&C), intrauterine injection of hypertonic saline solution (salting out), hysterectomy, and prostaglandin infusion.[18] D&C is most commonly used in first trimester abortions. In many hospitals in Africa, it is also used for the management of incomplete abortion arising mainly out of the crude methods previously discussed. The procedure is performed in theater under general anesthesia or heavy sedation. The cervical muscle ring is first paralyzed and dilated or stretched open. A curette, a loop-shaped steel knife, is then inserted into the uterus. The surgeon then scrapes the uterine wall, dismembering the developing fetus and scraping the placenta from its attachment on the wall of the uterus. This procedure usually leads to profuse bleeding. Forceps are used to remove the various parts of the embryo's body, which attending nurses are expected to count to make sure no part remains inside the womb.

The alternative to the dilation and curettage method is a vacuum aspiration or suction abortion in which, after the cervix is dilated, a powerful

17. Family Planning Association of Madagascar, "Maternal and Child Health," 54.

18. Davis, *Abortion and the Christian*, 27–29; Rogo et al., "Induced Abortion," 18; Grassian, *Moral Reasoning*, 244–45; and Boss, *Birth Lottery*, 95.

suction tube attached to a suction apparatus is inserted into the uterus. The body of the developing embryo or fetus is sucked out into a jar, being crushed or torn in the process. It works like a vacuum cleaner. The head of the fetus is sometimes crushed if it is too large to be sucked out of the womb. Some physicians scrape the uterus afterwards as a precaution against any fetal tissue remaining behind. Before the late 1970s when vacuum aspiration became a preferred method for doctors, dilation and curettage was the most common abortion method.

Saline abortion involves salt poisoning of the fetus in the second trimester. A long needle is inserted through the abdomen into the woman's womb. The needle extracts about eight ounces of amniotic fluid, replacing it with a highly concentrated salt solution. The fetus breathes in the salt solution and is poisoned by it. The concentrated saline solution burns off the outer layer of the baby's skin and causes brain hemorrhages. It takes about one hour for the child to slowly and painfully die by this method. Then eight to seventy-two hours later the mother goes into labor and delivers a dead baby. Grassian observes that, occasionally, the fetus survives the salt solution and emerges alive.[19] Such a baby is usually abandoned to die of neglect. In order to prevent the occurrence of such live births, a program has been initiated offering fetal intra-cardiac potassium chloride injection as an adjunctive measure.[20]

A hysterectomy abortion is the least often used method of late-term abortions, and may be performed if the pregnancy is too advanced for the D&C or salting out procedures. It poses the greatest danger to the woman and is the most likely to result in a live baby. The technique is similar to that of a Caesarean section, except that the incisions made in the abdomen are smaller. After the child is removed from the womb, it is laid aside to die from neglect. In effect it may lead to infanticide. More recently, prostaglandin infusions have been introduced as abortifacients. These are hormone-like substances, which artificially induce labor. They may be administered orally, intravenously, by vaginal suppositories, or by direct injection into the amniotic sac. The child is frequently born alive, but is too small to survive.

The detailed description of termination of pregnancy or abortion procedures provides the reader with information on the causes, conditions, procedures and consequences. These in turn help the reader to appreciate the necessity of a clear, consistent and effective articulation of an ethical

---

19. Grassian, *Moral Reasoning*, 245.
20. Callahan, "Ensuring a Stillborn," 254.

theory for its members. Whether carried out in a crude way or as a medical procedure, termination of pregnancy involves loss of blood, pain and the killing of human life. It is recommended that a mandatory explanation of the factual details of abortion be given to women to enable them to make an informed choice.

CONSEQUENCES OF ABORTION

It appears that, whether done by crude methods or by medical procedures, abortion has certain consequences, which cannot be ignored in a study of the ethical challenges of the problem. Any procedures carried out on the human body that result in interference with human life and health poses moral challenges. In order to judge either the wrongness or the rightness of pregnancy termination, it is important that its physical and psychological consequences be examined. Reports, from other parts of the world in general and Africa in particular, of the effects of pregnancy termination are relevant and replicable to the Kenyan situation.

The Family Planning Association of Madagascar reports that in 1988 there were 8,934 cases of illegally induced abortion that ended up in hospitalization; out of that number, 166 patients died.[21] Sai cites post-abortion infertility, ectopic pregnancy, and hysterectomy as major consequences of improperly terminated pregnancies.[22] Andre Jules Passé says that, in Burkina Faso, the immediate complications of unsafe pregnancy termination include steady hemorrhaging, which may necessitate blood transfusion, retention of ovular residue, which is quite common and is responsible for hemorrhages and infections, and cervical vaginal wounds, which arise from the use of potassium permanganate suppositories. During dilation and curettage, perforations of the uterine walls occur, and death is caused by hemorrhaging, pelviperitonitis with septicaemia, renal failure and hepatitis.[23]

The abortion patient in Africa is reportedly notorious for going for treatment late. This lateness, delay in hospital while waiting for attention, together with the unhygienic conditions under which most of these inductions are performed lead to a higher frequency of medical complications than reported elsewhere. Septicaemia, hemorrhage, and trauma are the

21. Family Planning Association of Madagascar, "Maternal and Child Health," 53.
22. Sai, "Overview of Unsafe Abortion," 2.
23. Passé, "State of Unsafe Abortion," 67.

commonest and most serious complications reported in African studies.[24] Lacerations may lead to difficulties in conceiving, and complication in future pregnancies. Fifty percent of all abortions lead to womb complications, which may lead to the impossibility of conceiving again.[25] Thiroux points out that a termination of pregnancy involves an intrusion into the woman's vagina and womb that introduces medical and psychological dangers to her body.[26] Medical dangers are those that develop as a result of the medical procedures of abortion. For instance, the dilation and curettage may lead to infections and, sometimes, to uterine perforations during the scrapping of the fetus and placenta. This may lead to excessive bleeding and death.

In his article "Facts Abortionists Ought to Consider," Dave Kahara mentions ectopic pregnancies and severe damage of the brain and nervous system as resultant injuries from anesthetic misadventure. He reports that 2 or 3 percent of aborting women suffer perforations of the uterus. Cervical lacerations may lead to cervical incompetence, premature delivery and labor complications. Cervical damage and scarring of the endometrium from abortion may, according to Kahara, increase the risk of abnormal development of the placenta in subsequent pregnancies, thus increasing the risk of birth defects. Besides, the risk of breast, cervical, ovarian and liver cancer is more than double in women who have had at least one abortion. There is also the risk of placenta previa, which Kahara describes as follows:

> Placenta previa involves a placenta being superimposed upon the os, and causes severe hemorrhage during labor. Abortion increases the risk of this condition by a factor of from 700 to 1,500 percent. Placenta previa also increases the risk of subsequent fetal malformation and perinatal death.[27]

Additionally, pelvic inflammatory disease and endometriosis, the inflammation of the endometrium, are also common physical effects on the woman who aborts.

Anthony Fisher equates Britain's abortion rate of 180,000 per year to a third of the total of British casualties in the Second World War. He decries this huge scale of killing the youngest members of the species, family, or community.[28] Although death is increasingly rare in Britain as a result of

24. Rogo et al., "Induced Abortion," 18.
25. ADS 9–10, 3.
26. Thiroux, *Ethics*, 281.
27. Kahara, "Facts Abortionists Ought to Consider," 3.
28. Fisher, "What Abortion Is Doing to Britain," 415.

abortion, infections, bleeding, cervical incompetence, infertility and cancer are on the increase.[29] In the United States, where abortion has been legal for twenty-one years, abortion is the sixth leading cause of maternal deaths.[30] Stott says that in America over 4,250 pregnancies were terminated daily, 177 hourly, or three every minute. In Washington, DC, abortions outnumbered live births by three to one at the time.[31]

Abortion's social consequences have been noted in some parts of the world. Jo Ann Downs reports that a survey that was done in a dozen villages in India showed that out of a population of 10,000 only 50 were girls. Pregnancies were monitored and female fetuses were always aborted because parents preferred male children.[32] Data from six clinics in Bombay showed that out of 8,000 amniocentesis tests indicating females, only one was carried to term.[33] In Korea, Downs reported that male births exceed female births by 14%. It was also forecasted that in Guangdong province in China, 500,000 bachelors would never marry because men in the 30 and 45 age group outnumbered women by more than ten to one.[34] For reasons such as these, Alice Paul, an ardent feminist who drafted the original version of the Equal Rights Amendment of the US Law, referred to abortion as "the ultimate exploitation of women."[35]

The effect of abortion is not only physical, but also economic. Franklin Payne argues that babies, children and the adults they become are a source of knowledge and wealth for a society. He refutes the general thought that the larger the population the fewer the resources available per capita. Drawing attention to the volume of goods and services necessary to raise the children to adulthood, he explains:

> Pregnant women have to have special clothes and medical care. Babies and children need clothes, food and bigger houses. When they enter school, they need supplies and teachers. All these items create industries and jobs for large numbers of people. . . . Then, when they marry and have their own children, they compound the

---

29. Ibid., 416.
30. Downs, "Opposing Abortion," 50.
31. Stott, *Issues Facing Christians Today*, 282.
32. Downs, "Opposing Abortion," 48.
33. *Newsweek*, 13 February, 1989.
34. *Time*, special fall ed., 1990, 40.
35. Downs, "Opposing Abortion," 49.

goods and services necessary. As they enter the work force, they become producers.[36]

Allan Carlson recalls that, in the 18th century, Thomas Malthus made a prediction that caused concern among social planners and economists. Malthus had warned that the earth's population would soon outstrip its resources, causing many to die of starvation. Carlson's reaction to Malthus' prediction is a calculation of the lost economic productivity of aborted children, assuming that the current numbers of abortions continue in the United States. In his essay, "The Malthusian Budget Deficit," Carlson figures out 20% in federal taxes and concludes that, a total of US$ 291 billion would be lost in taxes by the year 2010. In the year 2025 the projected economic value of the aborted children would have totaled US$ 1.45 trillion in that year alone.[37] This is an irony in pregnancies being terminated because of their financial liability to families. If Carlson's projections are accurate, then, abortions lead to a considerable loss of human and economic resources to any nation.

Physical and economic effects aside, abortion has a heavy emotional, psychological effect on the woman who does it. The one positive effect is the immediate relief that one is no longer burdened with an unwanted pregnancy.[38] Some studies have reported that abortion has sometimes functioned as a stress reliever whose negative outcome was minimal.[39] Michels, Sappington, Van der Spuy, and Kahara all agree that post-abortion syndrome (PAS) is the most significant and predominant psychological effect of abortion on women.[40] PAS is a valid syndrome characterized by distinct patterns and is usually diagnosed as post-traumatic stress disorder (PTSD). PAS was first officially recognized by the American Psychiatric Association (APA) in 1980, and occurs when women repress the grief that results from the loss of their aborted child. Michels provides an exhaustive list of the emotional reactions which a woman suffering from PAS might experience:

> . . . depression, grief, anxiety, sadness, shame, helplessness, hopelessness, sorrow, lowered self-esteem, distrust, hostility towards self and others, regret, insomnia, recurring dreams, nightmares,

---

36. Payne, *Biblical Healing for Modern Medicine*, 115.
37. Carlson, "Malthusian Budget Deficit," 35.
38. Michels, *Helping Women Recover from Abortion*, 29.
39. Van der Spuy, "Post-Abortion Syndrome," 141.
40. Michels, *Helping Women Recover*, 30, Sappington, "Abortion," 189, Van der Spuy, "Post-Abortion Syndrome," 143, and Kahara, "Facts Abortionists Ought to Consider," 3.

> anniversary reaction, suicidal behavior, alcohol and/or chemical dependencies, sexual dysfunction, insecurity, numbness, painful re-experiencing of the abortion, relationship disruption, communication impairment, isolation, fetal fantasies, self-condemnation, flashbacks, uncontrollable weeping, eating disorders, preoccupation, distorted thinking, bitterness, and a sense of loss and emptiness.[41]

To this apparently exhaustive list Sappington adds the problems of guilt and anger.[42] Women who abort have more psychological problems than those who carry their pregnancies to term and, according to Kahara, can be expected to require psychiatric help up to eight times more frequently. Twenty percent of women who abort consider suicide at some time, and one quarter are heavily dependent on alcohol. Other symptoms cited by Kahara include flashbacks, hysterical outbreaks, and loss of pleasure during sexual intercourse.[43]

The woman's reexperiences of the abortion may occur in at least one of a number of ways. These may include recurrent memories of the abortion or the unborn child, and the sudden feeling as if the abortion were reoccurring. As Michels explains, the woman may see herself lying on the procedure table and watch as the abortionist vacuums or suctions her baby out through the tube. The terror and pain she felt during the abortion will be as real in her mind as it was the day of the abortion.[44] She may also experience an avoidance phenomenon, shown by a marked diminished interest in her personal life, a sense of detachment from others, a reduced ability to feel or express emotions and increased hostile reactions.[45] Van der Spuy laments that "the grief-stricken cry of the mother (the second victim of abortion) is difficult to hear above the clamor of the abortion debate."[46] He, however, calls for a balance in the use of factors related to PAS. While it would be unacceptable to generalize or to imply that all women who have abortions will suffer from PTSD, there should not be a reluctance to point out the negative consequences of abortion for fear of providing support to anti-abortion groups.

41. Michels, *Helping Women Recover*, 30–31.
42. Sappington, "Abortion," 189.
43. Kahara, "Facts," 3.
44. Michels, *Helping*, 31.
45. Ibid., 32.
46. Van der Spuy, "Post-Abortion Syndrome," 142.

Women may be discouraged from revealing their post-abortion feelings, if the negative effects of abortion are either overemphasized or underemphasized. This may, in turn, prevent them from receiving the counseling, care, and support they need. Van der Spuy however, points out that, when exposed to events that either symbolize or resemble the abortion experience, nightmares or distress may occur in women who have aborted. Such symbols may include subsequent pregnancies, the anniversary of the abortion, seeing other pregnant women, babies, children of potentially the same age as the aborted child, vacuum cleaners, and doctor's offices.[47] Abortion also affects the psychological relationship between the mother and her other children. Van der Spuy describes the problem:

> The mother can either be enmeshed or can inadequately bond with future children because: she is afraid something bad will happen to them; she is afraid that they will be taken away; she feels undeserving of intimacy, she fears that bonding will be seen as disloyalty to her aborted child; she may cast the other child into "a replacement baby" and become enmeshed; she might become overprotective; she might have unrealistic expectations—expecting them to make up for the lost life of the aborted child.[48]

It also appears that, where an abortion is not discussed and is kept as a "family secret," division and emotional distancing occurs between the woman and her family of origin. For a Christian woman, she may feel estranged from God and the church.

Electing to have an abortion is a difficult decision for a woman, usually made under severe pressure. But once she has decided to have it, the woman will normally develop some defense mechanisms. Michels recounts four of the defense mechanisms as: rationalization—the reasons a woman gives for having an abortion that explains that what she has done is good; suppression—when a woman erases any negative feelings about abortion from her mind; repression—when the woman is not aware of any negative feelings she may have about the abortion; and compensation—when the woman becomes pregnant soon after abortion to make up for the lost child.[49]

The psychological effects of abortion have been reported among nurses and doctors who carry them out. Warren M. Hern and Billie Corrigan

---

47. Ibid., 143.
48. Ibid., 144.
49. Michels, *Helping*, 41.

are former Chief Physician and Head Nurse respectively at the Boulder Abortion Clinic in the US. In 1978 they reportedly presented a paper entitled "What About Us? Staff Reactions on Abortion," in which they said that eight of the fifteen staff members surveyed reported emotional problems. Two said they worried about the physician's psychological well-being. Two reported horrifying dreams involving fetuses, one of which involved the hiding of fetal parts so that other people would not see them. Hern and Corrigan went on to conclude:

> We have produced an unusual dilemma. A procedure is becoming recognized as the procedure of choice in late abortion, but those capable of performing or assisting with it are having strong personal reservations about participating in an operation, which they view as destructive and violent.[50]

Some doctors and nurses have had to deal with such emotional trauma through the use of alcohol (too much drinking) and taking of drugs. Others have committed suicide.[51] Okullu discusses the dilemma of nurses who take part in abortion operations:

> Disposing of a recognizable baby, however small, is a wretched business for a young girl (nurse) whose chosen vocation is the preservation of life. There is a dilemma for a nurse who has to throw away an aborted fetus alive because the mother does not want it, and do all in her power to save the life of another child because the mother wants it.[52]

The reality is such that doctors who do the operation, and nurses who assist, must live with the memory of the experience. Okullu further notes that, sometimes, patients suffering from other illnesses and are on need of urgent attention may have to wait while the doctor performs an abortion to get rid of a life.[53] Such difficult experiences cause emotional stress in doctors and nurses who, like the women who abort, need the church's intervention with a theological-ethical response that affirms human dignity.

---

50. Green, *Last Days Newsletter*, 30.
51. Ibid.
52. Okullu, *Church and Marriage*, 54.
53. Ibid., 55.

SUMMARY

This chapter has provided a review of the causes, procedures and consequences of termination of pregnancy, thereby giving the reader an understanding of the problem of termination of pregnancy. The chapter discusses the magnitude of the problem and identifies the human dignity gaps that have persistently left the problem largely unresolved in Kenya. The missing link continues to be the issue of human dignity as an aspect that may help develop a resolution to the problem. The causes of pregnancy termination, as discussed, reveal situations that degrade the dignity of both the pregnant woman and the unborn fetus she carries. The procedures by which pregnancies are terminated seem to show marks of disregard for the dignity of the pregnant woman and her fetus. The consequences, too, appear to show a deep need for recourse to a quest for human dignity. This makes this research necessary, as it seeks to integrate the aspect of human dignity into the ethical challenge of termination of pregnancy in the Kenyan context.

CHAPTER 4

THEORETICAL AND CONCEPTUAL FRAMEWORK

THEORETICAL FRAMEWORK

Christian Ethics in Context

Discussions on the problem of termination of pregnancy characteristically raise different viewpoints, which are based on various ethical theories. Such ethical theories are so strong in their foundations that objections from others do not achieve much in seeking to get to a solution to the problem. However, this research notes that each ethical theory is seriously limited in scope, and not one ethical theory can offer adequate solutions to the problem. It also hereby judged unfair that the failure to find a solution be blamed on the perceived inadequacy of one ethical theory. Instead, the research proposes that a theory of compromise be developed and applied to resolve the problem.

Christian ethics, by its very nature, is religious. The limitation of any religious injunction is that it rests on authority, and as Pojman points out, "We are not always sure of or in agreement about the credentials of the authority, nor how the authority would rule in ambiguous or new cases."[1]

1. Pojman, *Ethical Theory*, 4.

And since religion is founded not on reason but on revelation, one cannot use reason to convince anyone who does not share one's religious views that yours are the right ones. It seems clear that both anti-abortion and pro-choice advocates often agree that it is wrong to kill innocent persons, but differ on specifics. Whereas an anti-abortion advocate may hold strongly to a religious view that states that the fetus has an eternal soul and thus a right to life, a pro-choice advocate may deny that anyone, leave alone a fetus, has a soul and maintain that only self-conscious, rational beings have a right to life.[2] Such differences cause us to go deeper in our discussion into the essence of our social existence. The purpose of this study is to secure valid principles of conduct and values that can be instrumental in guiding human actions and producing good human relationships with regard to termination of pregnancy.

In the Christian faith, ethics and theology are very closely related. Christian behavior is linked to Christian belief in the LORD Jesus Christ. Faith in Christ produces the inner motivation of an individual's love for God and commitment to following Christ. The result is seen in the Christian's love for the neighbor. But this is easier said than done, for belief does not always lead to practice. Geoffrey W. Bromiley discusses three problems in the relationship between doctrine and ethics. The first problem is that ethics deals with visible acts and not just inner motivations. A Christian may well do anything that a non-Christian does. Such an act can, by itself, be the subject of an independent study, which may create room for ethics to operate as an autonomous discipline without theological influence. The second issue is that the Christian beliefs, which underlie Christian conduct, are not totally different from religious beliefs that are foundational to non-Christian ethical systems.[3] This makes a comparative study of ethical systems and values possible and "Christian ethics can be subsumed under general ethical and philosophical investigation."[4] Third, Christian conduct does not consistently or absolutely express the revelation, which provides its ultimate motivation. Instead, doctrinal expressions undergo cultural and intellectual assimilation in the form of contextualization. Whenever this happens, ethics breaks from theological study to merge into a more general inquiry.

---

2. Ibid.

3. *International Standard Bible Encyclopaedia*, s.v. "Ethics and Dogmatics" (2:187).

4. Ibid.

The validity of the problems raised by Bromiley notwithstanding, it remains appropriate to study biomedical ethical issues within the theological context. Theology, in Tité Tienou's thought, is "the reasoned statement of biblical revelation, in specific places and specific times, which makes possible the transmission of the Christian faith to the future generations."[5] He compares the Christian faith to a beautiful song:

> Biblical revelation forms the words of the song and theology represents the music and the rhythm. Both revelation and theology are needed. In our cultures, music and rhythm serve to support the transmission and instruction of the messages. Likewise, theology is the indispensable support of the revealed Word of God.[6]

A Christian ethical theory has to draw from the vast resources of biblical theology in order to adequately facilitate a Christian ethical approach to biomedical problems, such as abortion. Threats to Christian theology, such as syncretism, in effect turn out to be threats to Christian ethics also. D. H. Field says that the fundamental ethical demand in Scripture is to imitate God.[7] The concern of a Christian ethical theory is to relate a theologically accurate understanding of God to the conduct of human beings. A similar thought is reflected in R. E. O. White:

> In contrast with philosophical systems, the enduring marks of biblical ethics are its foundation in relationship with God; its objective, imposed obligation to obedience; its appeal to the deepest in man; its down-to-earth social relevance; and its capacity for continual adaptation and development.[8]

The task of the Christian ethicist is to identify an ethical theory, which does not negatively compromise the truthfulness of the Word of God, while at the same time having the potential of a sympathetic application in individual moral struggles of modern human life. A Christian ethical theory derives its moral data from the Bible, which is the Christian's final, infallible, authoritative revelation of God's will for humanity. When in doubt about the correct solution of a moral problem, or when attempting to justify a moral belief, the Christian must make reference to biblical directives, or principles derived thereof. Christian ethics is, therefore, absolutist

---

5. Tienou, *Theological Task of the Church in Africa*, 12.
6. Ibid.
7. Field, "Abortion," 232.
8. White, "Biblical Ethics," 377.

in character, since the Christian moral standards depend on God for their validity. Ethical principles derive their validity from the fact that God has commanded them. Consequently, morality is based on divine will, not on independently existing reasons for action. But absolutes, if applied without due regard to human experience, may cause more damage. So a theory of compromise that integrates graded absolutism is proposed as both realistic and sympathetic to human experience.

Absolutism

Ethical absolutism is an ethical theory based on the principles that moral values are imperatives, which human beings have to live by in total obedience. Christian ethics generally defines "good" as what God wills, and his will is absolute, based on his unchangeable moral character. In Leviticus 11:45 God demands holiness from his people, saying, "Be holy because I am holy." Jesus taught his disciples in Matthew 5:48, "Be perfect, therefore, as your heavenly Father is perfect."

As an ethical theory for Christians, absolutism has been widely discussed by Norman L. Geisler, who argues that if an absolutely morally perfect God exists, then by his very nature he is the ultimate standard for what is good and what is not.[9] Since God's moral character does not change (Mal 3:6; Jas 1:17), it follows that moral obligations flowing from his nature are absolute. They are always binding everywhere on everyone. Geisler further explains that Christian ethics is based on God's commands,[10] the revelation of which is both general (Rom 1:19–20; 2:12–15) and special (Rom 2:18; 3:2).

God has revealed himself both in nature (Ps 19:1–6) and in Scripture (Ps 19:7–14). God's commands for all people are to be found in general revelation, while his will for believers is declared in special revelation. In both cases, divine revelation forms the basis of human ethical conduct. Ethical absolutism, as proposed by Geisler, takes three forms, namely, unqualified absolutism, conflicting absolutism, and graded absolutism.

Unqualified absolutism is thought to be the most influential and widely held view among Christians, and teaches that absolute moral principles never conflict.[11] All moral conflicts are only apparent, not real, and sin is

---

9. Geisler, *Christian Ethics*, 21.
10. Ibid., 23.
11. Ibid., 79.

always avoidable. One proponent of unqualified absolutism was Immanuel Kant who called the universal moral obligation a categorical imperative. By that expression he meant that duty was unconditional, not conditional.[12] Kant believed that moral duties, by their nature, admitted no exceptions, since any exception to a moral law would indicate that it was not truly a rule. He urged people to treat others as an end, and never as a means to an end.

This form of absolutism acknowledges that we live in a fallen world, and in such a world real moral conflicts do occur. Whenever two duties conflict, a person is morally responsible for both duties. God's law can never be broken without guilt. In such cases, one must simply do the lesser evil, confess his sin, and ask for God's forgiveness. Helmut Thielicke said, "I can reach such a decision only by going through the conflict and enduring it, not by evading it in the name of some kind of perfectionism."[13] The theory of conflicting absolutism is based on the biblical teaching that not all sins are equal. In John 19:11, Jesus said to Pilate, "The one who handed me over to you is guilty of a greater sin." In fact, one sin is so bad that it is unpardonable—the blasphemy against the Holy Spirit (Matt 12:32). Geisler summarizes the thought: "Whenever our moral duties conflict, we should obey the greater one, realizing that breaking the other is a sin. Nonetheless, it is the lesser sin in the situation. It is always our responsibility to do our best, even when it is not good."[14]

The theory of graded absolutism has been variously referred to as ethical hierarchicalism, qualified absolutism and contextual absolutism. In agreement with conflicting absolutism, it teaches that moral conflicts exist. But it clarifies that there are greater and lesser commands, and that our responsibility is to obey the greater commands. Consequently, we are not guilty for not following the lesser commandment in conflict with the greater one.[15]

In Matthew 23:23, Jesus spoke of weightier matters of the law. He spoke of the "least" and "greatest" commandment (Matthew 22:36). He told Pontius Pilate that Judas Iscariot had committed the "greater sin" (John 19:11). Geisler explains, "Despite a rather widespread evangelical distaste for a hierarchy of sins (and virtues), the Bible does speak of the 'greatest'

12. Ibid., 83.
13. Ibid., 99.
14. Ibid., 102.
15. Ibid., 26.

virtue (1 Corinthians 13:13) and even of 'greater' acts of a given virtue (John 15:13)."[16] The Bible talks of degrees of punishment in hell (Matt 5:22; Rom 2:6; Rev 20:12), as well as graded levels of reward in heaven (1 Cor 3:11, 12), to indicate that moral obligations come in degrees. Some Christians' sins call for excommunication (1 Cor 5), while others call for death (1 Cor 11:30). Geisler discusses this further:

> Perhaps the clearest indication of higher and lower moral laws comes in Jesus' answer to the lawyer's question about the "greater commandment" (Matthew 22:34–39). Jesus clearly affirms that the "first" and "greatest" is over the "second," that loving God is of supreme importance, and then beneath that comes loving one's neighbor.[17]

In Matthew 10:37 Jesus says, "He who loves father or mother more than me is not worthy of me." Proverbs 6:16; 1 Timothy 1:15; 1 John 5:16; and Matthew 5:22 all support this point. Besides, two theories admit the truth of this same point. Conflicting absolutism speaks of the lesser evil, implying that not all evils are equal. Unqualified absolutism admits that moral laws are higher than civil or ceremonial laws commanded by God.[18]

In addition to all the strengths of conflicting absolutism, graded absolutism imputes no guilt for the unavoidable moral conflicts, provided one keeps the higher moral law. A just God will not hold anyone guilty for doing what is actually impossible. In the words of Geisler,

> In real, unavoidable moral conflicts, God does not hold a person guilty for not keeping a lower moral law so long as he keeps the higher. God exempts one from his duty to keep the lower law since he could not keep it without breaking a higher law. This exemption functions something like an ethical "right of way" law.[19]

While avoiding the problem of legalism created by unqualified absolutism, graded absolutism seems to strike a balance with Fletcher's situationism. In graded absolutism, biblical commands against blasphemy, idolatry, adultery, murder, lying and so forth are absolute. Fletcher's situationism presents only one absolute, namely the law of love. While in situationism, the situation determines an individual's course of action, graded absolutism

---

16. Ibid., 116.
17. Ibid.
18. Ibid., 117.
19. Ibid., 120.

only takes note of situational factors to help discover what God has determined to be done. Situational factors help one discover which command of God is to be applied in a specific case.

In applying graded absolutism to termination of pregnancy, it is necessary to list down and rank all the sins, problems, and obligations related to the problem. Since it may be deduced that the Bible upholds the absolute sanctity of life for both the fetus and the mother, it may be a greater command to preserve the mother's life without imputing guilt for the resultant death of the fetus. There may be a conflict between the principle that upholds the sanctity of life, and the one that commands Christians not to promote human suffering. This may be in a case where a woman is pregnant with a severely deformed fetus. The higher moral law here may be to preserve human life, the fetus, and in the process promote human suffering to both mother and child. There may be no guilt imputed on the mother for letting a disabled child live. The human suffering experienced in pain, body deforming or material and financial deprivation are not good experiences. The Christian, in applying graded absolutism, needs to consider what would be a lower moral and what would be higher in each case.

In this research, graded absolutism is integrated with the theory of compromise in order to effectively address the issues around the problem of termination of pregnancy. In order to integrate the graded absolutism with compromise, it is necessary to review the theory of compromise as discussed by Martin Benjamin.[20]

Moral Compromise

Christian ethics is marked by great diversity, and a thinker can support a particular perspective as the most satisfactory Christian solution to an issue, such as termination of pregnancy. Christian ethics should not be a monolithic reality where a particular formulation of any ethical question is the only legitimate expression of the Christian faith. In this thesis God is viewed, not merely as the source of authority for certain laws, but as "one who acts in history with freedom of the faithful man to meet contingent situations in fidelity to him without bondage to law." Jesus Christ is herein seen to portray the love of God in redeeming men so that they can respond to the world about them in the freedom of their own situation. In this spirit, the position herein taken is that God is not exclusively served in churches

20. Benjamin, *Splitting the Difference*.

and monasteries. Service in what are commonly termed "secular vocations" and what Christians generally do as "worldly chores" are means within which humanity serves God. These include intellectual pursuits in which ethical theories may be developed for solving human moral dilemma.

To glean ideas and principles from various sources and integrate them to complement each other in dealing with an ethical issue requires the Christian to compromise. Although in some degree everyone does compromise, the idea is very much disliked by many contemporary Christian scholars.

The compromise theory is described by Martin Benjamin as one in which "integrity is not only compatible with a certain amount of compromise but that in the modern world the preservation on integrity will occasionally require compromises of a certain sort."[21] Judgment is to be carefully exercised because compromise is likened to fire which is both necessary and dangerous to human life: not to be always accepted, lest we become alienated from ourselves; and not always to be rejected, lest we cut ourselves off from large sections of our society.[22] Benjamin further explains:

> We often lack the time, money, energy, and other human and natural resources to satisfy everyone's rights or interests, let alone their wants and desires. And when rights or interests conflict because of scarcity, compromise may seem to be both necessary and appropriate. Factual uncertainty, moral complexity, the need to maintain a continuing co-operative relationship, the need for a more or less immediate decision or action, and a scarcity of resources constitute the circumstances of compromise.[23]

In other words, we may know of ethically absolute principles; we may even believe those principles. But reality dawns on us when conflicts occur, based on what is actually on the ground, and compromise becomes the only realistic option.

As Benjamin points out, circumstances of compromise comprise of "factual uncertainty, moral complexity, the need to maintain a continuing cooperative relationship, the need for a more or less immediate decision or action, and a scarcity of resources."[24] There may be circumstances in which a pregnancy is surrounded by similar demands, and moral compromise

21. Ibid., 2.
22. Ibid., 3.
23. Ibid., 32.
24. Ibid.

may be the best possible way forward. Such compromise is evident in the more conservative abortion policies which, while emphasizing the fetus's right to life, often allow for what appear to be inconsistent exceptions for pregnancy due to rape or incest.[25] Compromise addresses ethical conflict in borderline situations. Chris Jones, in attempting to link compromise to the problem of euthanasia, explains:

> In life borderline situations are given—meaning that there is often a conflict in obligations within a specific situation. Once such a situation has developed it cannot be avoided or wished away. One is forced to make a decision. This decision must always aim at causing the least suffering and damage, but at the same time demonstrating the most love. This choice which has to succeed in defusing the conflict within a given situation is called compromise. And it differs from consensus.[26]

Jones maintains that no guilt attaches to the kind of compromise which expresses the choice of a greater good. This is the context in which people in Scripture who compromised by telling lies in order to save lives, like the Hebrew midwives (Exod 1:15) and Rahab the prostitute (Josh 2:1–7), are praised, and not called to repentance.

In discussing the compromise theory in relation to the challenge of termination of pregnancy, Benjamin explains three main positions on the issue as the extreme conservative position, the extreme liberal position and the moderate position. For the extreme conservative, human life begins at conception and all living human beings (both prenatal and postnatal) are, or should be, equally protected by laws against killing. The extreme liberal, however, argues that a necessary condition for having the right to life is a personal interest in continued life, which requires developed capacities for self-awareness and a sense of the future, capacities which emerge at or sometime after birth. Falling between these two is the moderate position in which the fetus acquires independent moral standing after conception but before birth. In these three positions, the status of the fetus remains

---

25. Ibid., 40. The idea is discussed elaborately by Thomas H. Murray in "So Maybe It's Wrong: Should We Do Anything about It?," in Weil and Benjamin, *Ethical Issues at the Outset of Life*, 239–57. Where abortion is prohibited unless a pregnancy comes about through rape or incest, Murray asks, "What makes these reasons more persuasive than others? If the fetus is truly an innocent person, then surely the fact that it came into existence through rape or incest is not in any way its fault."

26. Jones, "Euthanasia," 1.

problematic.[27] When the extreme liberals maintain that "not all living human beings (for example fetuses, anencephalic infants, those in a persistent vegetative state, and perhaps some who are severely mentally handicapped or senile) are persons"[28] both human dignity and human equality are dealt a significant blow.

> To have one's dignity and worth as a person turn on having certain cognitive capacities—capacities that some humans might lack and some nonhumans, including some animals, might possess—is for many a final and wholly intolerable assault on a world view and way of life in which personhood is "a natural, inborn, and inherited right, rather than social, contingent, and assigned right."[29]

In view of the sharp differences, there is need to explore the plausibility of an integrity-preserving compromise on termination of pregnancy. Benjamin argues that a compromise might sufficiently diffuse the extreme rhetoric and tactics of those on the extreme positions.[30] He further suggests that "abortion seems more suited to political accommodation than constitutional law."[31] A plausible compromise in the challenge of termination of pregnancy ought to require concessions by both sides and be able to be seen by the opposing parties as somehow splitting the difference between them.

CONCEPTUAL FRAMEWORK

Following the recommendations of Chandran a conceptual framework has been designed for this research in order to present "a schematic representation of a research problem that includes a network of concepts (factors or

---

27. Benjamin, *Splitting the Difference*, 151–52. While making reference to Feinberg (1986:290), Benjamin points out that the extreme conservative position would require us to do as much to preserve the life of a newly fertilized ovum as for anyone else whose life is in danger. He reports that over 40% of fertilized ova fail to survive until implantation, and the spontaneous abortion rate after implantation ranges from 10% to 20%. If we seriously believe that the life of an embryo or a zygote is as valuable as that of any postnatal human being, we will have to commit as much money to preventing this loss of life as we now commit to preventing the deaths of persons after they are born. Yet this seems absurd.
28. Benjamin, *Splitting the Difference*, 159.
29. Ibid.
30. Ibid., 163.
31. Ibid., 165.

variables) and exhibits the flow and direction of their relationships."[32] The flow chart on the next page exhibits which concepts are related to which others. In this conceptual framework the six main variables are identified as theological-ethical framework, the church's understanding of human dignity, how the church responds to pregnancy (especially out of wedlock), decisions on termination of pregnancy, consequences of the decisions, and the possible development of a new theological-ethical framework in the church. The flow chart shows how each preceding variable relates to the succeeding one. The understanding is that the existing theological-ethical framework in the church, written or oral, shapes the church's understanding of human dignity, a factor that determines the church's response to the problem of termination of pregnancy. The church's response then influences how individuals decide what to do with pregnancies, leading to adverse consequences. A new theological-ethical framework can lead to new development, with positive outcomes.

---

32. Chandran, *Research Methods*, 61.

Theoretical and Conceptual Framework

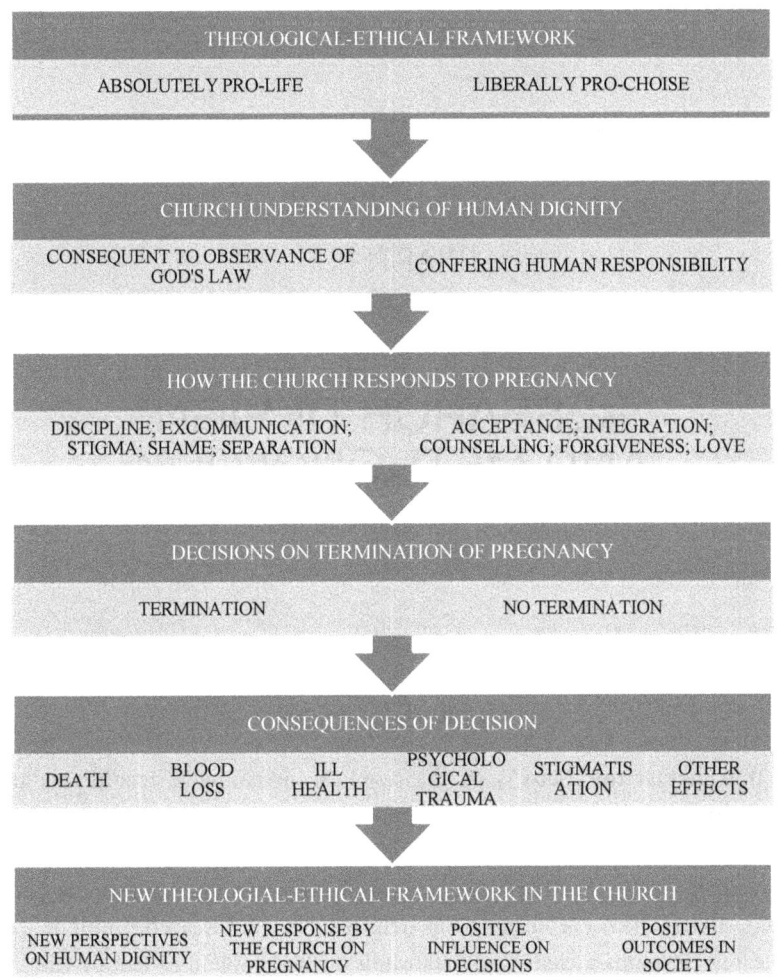

CHAPTER 5

RESEARCH DESIGN AND METHODOLOGY

INTRODUCTION

In this chapter the focus is on the research instruments, techniques and procedures, with due attention given to the population of study. It gives a description of the research design, the population of study, data collection procedures, as well as the research tools such as structure interview questions, all of which are designed to help resolve the research problem. The research develops a clear understanding of the problem of termination of pregnancy and to integrate the concept of human dignity into the church's theological-ethical response to the challenge.

Research is understood to mean "carrying out an enquiry or a critical examination of a given phenomenon diligently."[1] It also means "seeking, organizing, analyzing and interpreting data."[2] It also refers to the process of "looking again objectively at a people, a community, church events, and situations in order to find evidence and to establish a hypothesis or an answer to a research question."[3] Simply put, research is "to look for, examine,

1. Mugenda and Mugenda, *Research Methods*, 1.
2. Kasomo, *Research Methods*, 1.
3. Chandran, *Research Methods*, 4.

investigate or explore."[4] These descriptions of research point to critical evaluation of concepts, phenomena and data in order to find evidence and answers. In response to these general characteristics of research, this study will seek to establish the AIC understanding, teaching and response on the problem of termination of pregnancy, to integrate the concept of human dignity into the AIC response to the theological-ethical challenge of pregnancy termination, and to determine how the AIC response can be improved in light of the research findings. The research method that will be used in this study is qualitative research, which is concerned with phenomena and can be used to study human behavior, including attitudes and opinions. Qualitative research "provides descriptions and accounts of the processes of social interaction in natural settings."[5] The attitudes and opinions of Christians at various levels in the church are evaluated qualitatively from a theological-ethical perspective, with a focus on the quest for human dignity in the church.

RESEARCH DESIGN

In order to fulfill the objectives of any research, it is necessary to develop a suitable research design which, according to Kasomo, "spells out what type of methods to use . . . show where and how the study is going to be done."[6] As Kombo and Tromp describe research design,

> It is the glue that holds all of the elements in a research project together . . . the scheme, outline or plan that is used to generate answers to research problems . . . an arrangement of conditions for collection and analysis of data in a manner that aims to combine relevance with the research purpose. It is the conceptual structure within which research is conducted.[7]

Chandran summarizes the same thought in describing research design as "a means to achieve the research objectives through empirical evidence that is acquired economically."[8]

---

4. Kombo and Tromp, *Proposal and Thesis Writing*, 8.
5. Kasomo, *Research Methods*, 65.
6. Ibid., 97.
7. Kombo and Tromp, *Proposal and Thesis Writing*, 70.
8. Chandran, *Research Methods*, 68.

This research uses descriptive design which is a method of collecting information by interviewing or administering a questionnaire to a sample of individuals especially when seeking information about people's attitudes, opinions, and habits.[9] In applying the descriptive method to this study, the researcher describes the ethical challenges of termination of pregnancy as it is in Kenya today as well as how the church is currently responding. The research finds out from church leaders and members of the AIC church, as well as doctors and lawyers, what their perceptions, attitudes and opinions are on the problem on relation to their quest for human dignity. Information was collected through interviews about the attitudes, perceptions and opinions on the problem under research. In order to implement this, the researcher constructed questions that solicited the desired information. Bishops, pastors, elders, and members of selected local churches of the AIC in Kisumu County of Kenya were interviewed, in addition to those from other churches. Other professionals, such as doctors, lawyers and administrators, were also interviewed. Focused group discussions were also held with the elders and women group leaders. The data was then summarized to provide descriptive information. The selected AIC local churches were be Arina, Manyatta, Onjiko, Pap DCC comprising of Wasare, Urudi, Bungu, Moro, Ragen, Osuri, Kibwon, Miruka, Ombo, and Olwalo local churches.

RESEARCH PROCEDURE

Step 1: The problem investigated was identified as the quest for human dignity in termination of pregnancy. This was investigated in the context of a theological-ethical evaluation of the church's response in Kenya.

    Step 2: A conceptual hypothesis was formulated and stated as: Whereas treating women with dignity in the church resolves ethical issues related to termination of pregnancy, an approach generally denying women dignity in the church complicates the issues.

    Step 3: Factors that were treated, manipulated or handled in the study were the church, human dignity and termination of pregnancy.

    Step 4: Relevant literature was reviewed to show what others have said about termination of pregnancy. The literature reviewed included books, journal articles, newspaper reports, special documents, and academic theses.

---

9. Kombo and Tromp, *Proposal and Thesis Writing*, 71.

Step 5: A study design was established that identified the respondents in the study, their numbers and locations. The key respondents in the focus group discussions were Christians classified as leaders of youth, men and women groups in selected churches in Kisumu County in Kenya. In each church, a group was formed from youth, women or men to enable the researcher to establish the perception of the church leaders and members on the treatment of pregnancy. The study was carried out through structured interviews and focused group discussions.

Step 6: Data collection involved collecting information from Christian doctors and lawyers using structured interviews, as well as FGD.

Step 7: Data Analysis and Report Writing.

RESEARCH INSTRUMENTS

a. Structured Interview Questions

b. Focused Group Discussions with church elders, women and youth

POPULATION SAMPLE AND SIZE

The population from which information will be sought is selected on the basis of diversity, representation, accessibility and knowledge. The researcher chose to use non-probability sampling in order to benefit from the representativeness of the concepts in their varying forms. The sampling will be purposive non-probability sampling and will be used to obtain specific and general information on the approach of the church to the problem of termination of pregnancy in Kenya. From the sample population, the results of the investigation will be generalized to the target population, which is the entire Christian community in Kenya as represented by the members of the AIC.

The AIC is the largest evangelical protestant church in Kenya, with a membership of almost 5 million people worshipping in well over 4,000 local congregations. The denomination carries out its ministry through an administrative structure that devolves progressively from the National Office into areas, regions, districts, and local churches. Nyanza Area covers what administratively exists as Nyanza Province, with an extension into

Western Province. Nyanza Area, run by the Area Church Council (ACC), is composed of eight regions run by Regional Church Councils (RCC), namely, Upper Western Lake Region, Lower Western Lake Region, Kisumu City Region, Kisumu Region, Central Lake Region, Muhoroni Region, Nyakach Region, and South Nyanza Region. In each region, there is an average of ten districts administered by District Church Councils (DCC). Under each district there are several local churches run by Local Church Councils (LCC). The entire Nyanza Area has a total of 70 districts, 600 local churches, and a membership of about 18,000 Christians in total. This study will focus on selected local churches in Kisumu County, which is purposely chosen for the study because it is the stronghold of the AIC in Nyanza Area. Out of the eight regions, seven of them with almost 16,000 Christians are geographically located within Kisumu County alone. In each of the selected churches chosen, the sample population will consist of one pastor, five elders, ten male members and sixteen female members. Of the ten male members, five will be members of the youth between ages fifteen and thirty. Similarly, of the sixteen female members, ten will be youth between ages fifteen and thirty. This will ensure that out of the thirty-two respondents interviewed in each local church, a minimum of sixteen will be female, while at least fifteen will be youth. The sample population of females will be purposely higher so as to obtain more responses from them. This is because of the perception that termination of pregnancy is primarily a female-folk challenge. The total population targeted is a minimum of 320 Christians, which is 2% of the total number of Christians in the AIC churches in Kisumu County. The sample population will consist of members from AIC Arina, Manyatta, Onjiko, and Pap DCC comprising of Wasare, Urudi, Bungu, Moro, Ragen, Osuri, Kibwon, Miruka, Ombo, and Olwalo local churches.

DATA COLLECTION PROCEDURE

This study involved both primary data and secondary data. The primary data was collected from structured interviews, focused group discussions and church records. Secondary was collected from newspaper reports, journal articles and books. In the structured interviews, intense qualitative probe questions were asked to the respondents. In addition, focused group discussions gave chance for getting information on opinions, feelings and attitudes of Christians on the problem of termination of pregnancy in relation to the quest for human dignity in the church.

Research Design and Methodology

The collection of primary data was done through structured interviews to individuals and field visits to churches where focused group discussions were held. Questions were asked directly by the researcher, and answers were recorded as they came from the respondents. In order to retain the original responses from the groups and ensure accuracy of data, no attempt was made to alter or interpret the responses in the process of initial recording. The collection of secondary data was done through the study of books, journal articles, and newspaper reports. The information was studied and reference was made to relevant portions for further discussion and evaluation.

ETHICAL CONSIDERATIONS IN DATA COLLECTION

There are ethical considerations that are an integral part of practice in research. Kombo and Tromp outline some of them as: the need to ensure that the benefits of the research far outweigh the costs involved in doing it; maintaining confidentiality at all times; one should not get involved in changing the subject's behavior; one should obtain informed consent and be completely honest and open; a researcher should protect subjects physically and psychologically as well as explaining fully the research in advance in addition to debriefing subjects afterwards to tell them about the results of the research.[10] These ethical issues will be adhered to adequately and appropriately.

Before embarking on data collection, a consent form was developed in accordance with the sample obtained from the Faculty of Theology at the University of Stellenbosch. This ensured that the consent of the respondents is obtained before the structured interviews are carried out. Additionally, a research permit was obtained from the National Council of Science and Technology in Kenya. Since the research will be carried out in Kenya where affiliation is a mandatory requirement for research students coming from outside the country, this was officially arranged with the Ethical Review Committee of the Great Lakes University of Kisumu where the researcher was an employee at the time of the study. The respondents will all be carefully briefed and their consent obtained before the interviews are done. Copies of the documents were appended into the thesis.

---

10. Kombo and Tromp, *Proposal and Thesis Writing*, 107.

SUMMARY

In this chapter, critical issues have been explained that focus on research methodology, design, population sampling, data collection procedure, as well as ethical issues and procedures. This serves to give direction and structure to the rest of the research and the outcomes derived thereof. The next chapter will discuss data collection and evaluation.

CHAPTER 6

RESEARCH FINDINGS

INTRODUCTION

This chapter presents and discusses the results of the data collected through structured interviews and focused group discussions held with various groups in selected churches in Kisumu County in Kenya. The purpose of the study was to find out the opinions, perceptions and attitudes of Christians on the problem of termination of pregnancy, to critically review the quest for human dignity in the ethical challenge of the problem and to evaluate the church's approach in the light of theological ethics in order to make appropriate recommendations to the church. Data analysis involved categorizing, organizing and summarizing information collected from both the structured interviews and focused group discussions in order to get answers to the research questions of the study.

DATA COLLECTION PROCEDURE

In this research, only qualitative data analysis was employed in the public study which was carried out in the months of August, September and October of the year 2012. Information from the FGDs was collected through open discussions in which all the informants actively participated and gave open-ended responses to the questions. Data reduction was done through careful all-inclusive recording of the responses in each discussion session. From the objectives stated in chapter 1, responses were categorized to develop responses to the research questions, and the emerging issues were noted for discussion, evaluation, and conclusion.

Data was collected from FGDs held in fifteen AIC local churches located in various districts of Kisumu County involving separate groups of men, women, and youth (both male and female). Structured interviews also conducted to get information from selected church leaders, as well as doctors and lawyers. The church leaders were deliberately selected because of their positions of leadership, which makes them custodians of the church's doctrinal and moral teachings. The doctors and lawyers were chosen because of their perceived regular engagement with patients in relation to unplanned pregnancies or their termination. The information gathered was classified according to the questions asked, which formed subtopics describing various themes.

INFORMATION FROM STRUCTURED INTERVIEWS

Responses from Church Ministers

A total of sixteen church ministers were interviewed from a variety of churches, including Africa Inland Church, Anglican Church of Kenya, Roman Catholic Church, Seventh Day Adventist Church, Redeemed Gospel Church, Africa Brotherhood Church, Friends (Quakers) Church, Church of Christ in Africa, First Church of Christ the Scientist, Gospel Confirmation Centre, and Nairobi Pentecostal Church. Of the sixteen church ministers interviewed, two gave brief and generalized responses in which they emphasized biblical principles of chastity and faithfulness as the only ways of preventing unwanted pregnancy and abortion. Fourteen gave detailed answers, and stated that pregnancy was the work of God and the beginning of human life. A few explained that, although pregnancy out of wedlock was a direct result of sin, the pregnancy itself should still be seen as a good process which must be allowed and nurtured to grow. All the 14 church leaders who responded declared that termination of pregnancy was murder, which should not be legalized at all. Two blamed the modern women's rights movement for championing abortion as a right for women. All of them considered the life of the fetus as of great value before God, and protected by the law against murder. Of the fourteen respondents, four stated that abortion could not be allowed for any reason; while ten said it could be carried out to save a woman whose life was at risk. Of the ten, four said that only qualified medical doctors should determine the perceived risk of life.

In response to the question on how churches should handle girls or women who get pregnant out of wedlock while in the church membership, three suggested that such women be put under church discipline. One respondent explained that, in their church, lessons on moral life were provided to members twice a week. If a member got pregnant, she was dismissed from church fellowship immediately. Eleven respondents laid emphasis on counseling as a means to assisting the woman into right relationship with God, with the fetus, and with other people. While discipline would be carried out, counseling was viewed as the principal means of helping the women. Two respondents said that, in their churches, the children born out of wedlock were baptized. In one of the two, only the first child born out of wedlock was baptized, with subsequent ones only baptized when in danger of death. This was intended to encourage the lady to get married.

One respondent narrated two relevant experiences. His daughter got pregnant before marriage. He disciplined her, but took good care of her until she gave birth. When she got pregnant again, he encouraged her to get married. In another experience, his son was responsible for a girl's pregnancy, but refused to marry the girl. He, the church minister, sponsored the girl for a secretarial course, and fully educated the child she gave birth to. The child recently graduated from an accredited private university.

Two respondents urged that pregnant schoolgirls be expelled from school in order to warn other schoolgirls against sexual immorality. Twelve respondents, however, advised that such girls be given time off, in order to carry the pregnancy to term, give birth and nurse the infant, after which she should be encouraged and accepted back into the school system. The pregnant woman and her doctor, her pastor and her boyfriend, are the people to decide cases of intended abortions, according to two respondents. Four respondents indicated only the pregnant woman and her doctor; two suggested the involvement of parents, while three would leave it to the hospital's ethics committee. Three did not respond to the question.

All the church leaders who responded emphasized the need for proper education and counseling of the youth as the way forward in resolving the abortion problem in Kenya. Respondents urged both the church and the state to actively engage in providing the education. Two respondents urged the government to get strict in implementing the law prohibiting abortion.

Results from Doctors

A total of thirty-nine doctors were interviewed, out of which twenty-nine were male while ten were female. Of the twenty-nine male doctors interviewed, six were orally interviewed, while twenty-three responded by posting the questionnaire sheets to the researcher. Similarly, of the ten female doctors interviewed, three were orally interviewed, while seven posted the questionnaire sheets. There were twenty-five male and eight female gynecologists/obstetricians. There were two male general surgeons, one female pediatrician, two male and one female general physician. The ages of the respondents varied from thirty to fifty-three years.

It was observed that those orally interviewed responded with enthusiasm and were willing, sometimes eager to discuss the object's related issues not asked for in the questionnaire. These provided insights on how the problem of abortion was perceived. During the oral interviews, the interviewer created a context in which interviews were carried out at the respondent's office at the respondent's preferred time schedule. The interviewer utilized such communication techniques as clarification, paraphrasing, summarizing and probing. The interviewer wrote field notes based on information gathered during the interviews. Information from those who filed in the questionnaires was brief and varied, and was received as it came.

The researcher followed the normal procedures for conducting research in Kenya. A valid research permit was obtained from the National Council of Science and Technology, upon submission of the relevant application papers and research proposal. The structured interviews were carried out in Kisumu County, but extended to Nairobi and Machakos Counties to include doctors from Kenyatta National Hospital and Machakos General Hospital. In each location, the District Commissioner's office was visited and appropriate authorization and guidance was obtained. In each hospital, additional permission was obtained from the Research and Ethics Committee. In Kisumu City where it was impossible to get authority to interview doctors in any of the hospitals, the District Commissioner was of great assistance in providing a guide to various locations to interview doctors, lawyers and church leaders.

It was established that responses indicated a variation of opinion, without regard to age or years of service of the respondents. For instance, opinions on why abortion should be either legalized or prohibited varied across the various ages represented.

Doctors were quite generous with information on the medical implications of a pregnancy. There was a general agreement that pregnancy was a normal physiological development in the human female, and should not be perceived as a disease. Pregnancy causes a number of physiological changes in the woman. For instance, the cardiac output increases because the body needs a little more oxygen. Breasts become larger and tender in preparation for lactation. Due to hyper pigmentation, the linea alba on the abdomen darkens. Morning sickness, indicated by vomiting, occurs, and sometimes swelling takes place on the legs. Pregnancy is known to cause emotional and physical drain on the mother, and results in an increased nutritional requirement. A woman's reaction to a pregnancy depends on whether she wants it or not. Where it is wanted, it is viewed as an achievement, and results in joy. Where it is unwanted, it leads to a moody and anxious personality. The pregnancy's success or failure depends on marital status, socioeconomic factors, as well as clinical state.

A number of reasons were given as to why an abortion procedure may be performed. Diseases enumerated included cancer, hypertension, active lung tuberculosis, cardiac disease, and rheumatic heart disease. These may put the pregnant woman's life in serious jeopardy, such that if the pregnancy is not terminated, both the mother and child will die. Other factors were given as reasons, which may be medically considered in order to terminate a pregnancy, such as excessive bleeding caused by an abnormal placenta. Sometimes, the fetus's structures may not be compatible with normal life, such as severe Down's syndrome, headless fetus, extreme hydrocephaly, and congenital anomalies. Patients with chronic kidney failure, or those suffering from thyrotoxicosis (where the thyroid gland functions abnormally), as well as those with deep venus thrombosis, which results from slow blood flow, may have pregnancies medically terminated. Other respondents mentioned unsuitable maternal mental state and German measles. A few respondents mentioned AIDS, incest, and rape, as mitigating factors that may also lead to termination of a pregnancy.

All the respondents agreed that abortion should be only carried out by a well-trained gynecologist. One respondent confided that clinical officers were currently being trained on the procedures, although the Kenyan law allowed only qualified physicians to do it. The general agreement is for any medially indicated abortion to be performed by a person with adequate understanding of the anatomy of the birth canal and the physiology of pregnancies. A few respondents suggested that the agreement of three doctors should be legally required, although one insisted that this was already a requirement in cases of rape and incest.

There are a number of medical problems that may arise during or after an abortion. Almost all respondents mentioned excessive hemorrhaging (bleeding), shock, collapse, perforation of the uterus and or the gut, and residual remains. Death of the woman was mentioned as a possible consequence of either shock, or bleeding, or both. Almost all mentioned depression, guilt, infection, sepsis, trauma, ectopic pregnancy, frozen pelvis, tetanus, cervical incompetence, and genital tract injuries. Two respondents mentioned uterus contrition and death out of drug allergies. One respondent stated that no complications were expected at all if the procedure was carried out professionally in a hygienic condition. Another respondent said that in any medical procedure there were expectations of complications and risks. One other respondent said that an operation by a qualified person could minimize the problems, since such a qualified person was neither afraid nor in a hurry, and operated in sterile conditions.

Out of the ten female doctors interviewed, three stated that abortion should be legalized in order to minimize the illegal, life-threatening abortions currently taking place. One of the three said she would personally not agree to perform any abortion because of her strong beliefs in the sanctity of human life. Two of them said it should be legalized only under strict medical grounds. Five of them said it should remain prohibited in Kenya. Three of the five appealed to the sacredness of the life of the fetus, one said the liberalization of abortion would promote promiscuity, while one gave no reason. Among the male doctors, ten respondents said abortion should remain prohibited. While three of the ten suggested that it should strictly remain within the medical indications currently allowed by law, three described it as an evil and murderous act. Others feared that the legalization might lead to abuse. Two felt that Kenya was not ready in terms of infrastructure and personnel. Nineteen respondents said abortion should now be legalized, to make it safe and more accessible. Five of the eight simply gave reasons for legalizing abortion, three outlined strict conditions, such as, it should be done before the age of three months, in a registered hospital, and to be done by a trained physician. They also insisted that counseling be done before the procedure is done. In total, fifteen respondent doctors wanted abortion to remain prohibited, while twenty-four wanted it legalized.

On the question of how educational institutions should deal with girls or women who get pregnant out of wedlock while undergoing training, there was a general agreement that the woman should be granted leave of absence for, say, one year, after which she would be mandatorily readmitted for studies. This was the response of thirty-seven respondents, including all ten females. One respondent said they should be counseled and offered the option of abortion, while one did not respond to the question. This response is an indicator that the Education Act in the laws of Kenya needs to be revised in order to allow girls who get pregnant to continue with education after delivery.

There was a variety of opinions concerning who should decide in cases of disputes over an intended abortion. A few say it should be pregnant woman alone, other say the pregnant woman and her doctor, while others would want the church pastor to be involved. The hospital's ethics committee, courts of law, and parents were also cited. On how best the abortion problem can be handled, public education and adequate professional counseling were stated as the key issues.

Responses from Lawyers

Six lawyers interviewed were randomly chosen, and all of them said that abortion should remain prohibited. All the lawyers agreed that the fetus had a right to life, and the mother had a duty to keep the pregnancy. Termination of a pregnancy is not permitted in Kenya, except where the mental or physical health of the woman is threatened. Such threat has to be determined by medical experts. In Kenyan law, it is also a felony to make pregnancy or a fact of birth a secret. These are drawn from Caption 64 Section 227 of the Penal Code of the Laws of Kenya. Section 228 of the same code specifically addresses the subject, "Killing of an Unborn Child," and effectively pronounces unlawful pregnancy termination as a criminal offence for which an offender is liable to imprisonment for life. However, according to Section 240, a doctor who performs an operation on a pregnant woman or an unborn child, and an abortion results, is not guilty if all of the following conditions are obtained: If he performed the operation "in good faith"; if the operation was done with reasonable care and skill; if the operation was performed for the patient's benefit; and if the operation was done upon an unborn child for the preservation of the mother's life. The operation must be judged reasonable by peers, and must have regard for the mental and physical state of the patient at the time of the operation. One major problem here is that the term "child" is not defined in the Act. The term "child" is defined in the Children and Young Persons Act, Caption 141 Laws of Kenya, as an infant of ages between one minute after birth and seventeen years. Therefore, it could be logically argued that a fetus is not a person or child.

From the lawyer respondents, there is an agreement that pregnant girls should not be expelled from school. Instead they should be advised to withdraw from learning until after the nursing period. It is wrong to criminalize the pregnancy of unmarried girls. One respondent suggested that an institution should be created for unmarried mothers to avoid shame and social stigma. One respondent suggested the involvement of hospital ethics committee and pastors in the decision making process, but clearly ruled out courts of law, which he said that had no jurisdiction over morality. All the respondents agreed on the need for adequate counseling procedures for the youth in order to prevent unwanted pregnancies.

SUMMARY OF RESULTS

The problem of abortion raises great concern among church leaders, doctors, and lawyers, some of whom would like to see it legalized, while others would rather maintain the current status quo. Those who want abortion legalized have expressed concern over the number of deaths resulting from unsafe abortions, as well as the serious complications on reproductive health caused by back street abortions. They project that legalized abortion will avail safe and affordable abortion procedures to women, and generally improve women's reproductive health. Those who object to the legalization of abortion see it as murder. Some have cited the infrastructural unpreparedness of Kenya in handling safe abortions if legalized. Others think abortion proponents are only interested in client's money.

It has been observed that, apart from doctors, no other category of people interviewed want abortion legalized. Both pastors and lawyers interviewed want abortion to remain prohibited in law. They pointed to it as murder, and associated its legalization with the licensing of sexual promiscuity. Instead, they suggested, education and counseling be strengthened among the youth in order to prevent unwanted pregnancies. The attitude and perception of doctors may have been influenced by their constant exposure and contact with patients who suffer from unwanted pregnancies and abortion. They have grown sympathetic to the health problems facing women in such situations, hence their recommendation that abortion be legalized. The research establishes that there are some doctors, perhaps in the minority, whose recommendation for legalization may be motivated by potential monetary gain that may be made available through legalization of pregnancy termination.

Almost all respondents agree that educational institutions should not expel girls who get pregnant out of wedlock while in school. Instead, such girls should be given a break off from studies in order to give birth and nurture their infants. After a period of, say, one-year such student should be readmitted to continue with their studies. Criminalizing pregnancy is a factor, which forces some girls into termination of pregnancy in order to avoid expulsion from school.

INFORMATION FROM FOCUSED GROUP DISCUSSIONS

The focused group discussions (FGDs) were held with seven different groups categorized, with bracketed abbreviations, as follows:

- Manyatta Married Men   (MMM)
- Manyatta Young Men   (MYM)
- Manyatta Young Women   (MYW)
- Onjiko Married Men   (OMM)
- Onjiko Married Women   (OMW)
- Pap Young Men   (PYM)
- Pap Young Women   (PYW)

The results from the FGDs were analyzed in relation to the questions that guided the discussions.

Church Teachings on Termination of Pregnancy

All the respondents in all the FGDs reported that they had never heard any public teaching in the church on the subject of termination of pregnancy.

No church teaching or preaching is done that focuses on the topic. In OMW one respondent said that sometimes speakers at Christian youth camps (organized by the church) generally addressed topics on teenage sexuality, thereby mentioning abortion as a consequence of sexual sin. In MYM it was mentioned that the church's teaching was against abortion, as the church leaders publicly declared during the 2010 Kenyan Constitution debate and referendum. The FGDs that mentioned the church's stand against termination of pregnancy said they understood the basis of the teaching as the biblical commandment in Exodus 20:13, which states, "You shall not murder." The men in MMM noted that church leaders do not teach this topic because they either fear dealing with family issues, or simply lack the training necessary to handle such a complex topic. PYM stated that the church was shy to discuss the topic, and that the church only taught holiness and spirituality.

Despite the lack of teaching and preaching in the church about termination of pregnancy, respondents variously said that it is illegal; it is sin; it is murder; life is sacred and only God should terminate it; abortion happens mostly when there is pregnancy outside marriage; sometimes it happens in marriage; and it is directly against God's directive to the biblical patriarchs to have children and multiply. They explained that believers were supposed to read the Bible and get lessons from it, that God creates a new child through the union of a man and a woman, and he also takes the child away at his discretion. Things are in God's control, and need to be left as such. All the FGDs pointed out that it was important for the church to take the topic seriously and begin addressing it publicly and regularly. In OMW members said the church avoided teaching on the topic because it was controversial, while in OMM they said the church had abandoned teaching on moral issues affecting contemporary Christians. They (OMM) explained how modern life had changed greatly and American culture, where pregnancy termination was a woman's right, was slowly coming to Kenya. The influence of the West, especially through television, magazines and the Internet, had watered down African customs of chastity and it was now difficult to train children. This situation had led to negative results, including teenage pregnancy and abortion.

In the PYW one respondent reported of having heard her teacher of Christian Religious Education (CRE) in a church-sponsored school explaining that abortion had both advantages and disadvantages. For the advantages the teacher had said that abortion can be a way of dealing with pregnancy arising out of rape, and may be a form of birth control. Yet the disadvantages had outweighed the advantages: one can lose her life in the process; it destroys a woman's reproductive system; leads to childlessness; and may cause one to give birth to an abnormal baby. Another FGD (OMM) suggested the revival of older cultural practices in the church as a way of enhancing morality and cited the example of churches in Sudan where women are not allowed to sit together with men in any public gathering, including church services.

The OMW discussed the significance of relevant teaching in the church, and raised several issues that needed emphasis: it is important for Christians to learn to trust in God during times of hardship, like teenage pregnancy; teaching abstinence enhances prevention of teenage pregnancy and abortion; girls need to be consistently and regularly taught against pre-marital sexual relations. They noted that, in the AIM/AIC tradition, girls used to be taught how to keep purity, hence teenage pregnancy was uncommon. Whereas conscience tells a Christian what actions would be morally wrong, people have not been taught to take responsibility for their actions. One respondent expressed concern that there were certain ill-behaved boys whose main goal was to impregnate certain girls from certain Christian families, and that girls needed both protection and teaching. The FGD further pointed out that parents feared telling off their children on wrongful sexual behavior for fear of rebellion. With nostalgia, they described old traditional Luo cultural settings in which girls slept in the grandmother's hut where they received lessons on teenage purity, sexuality, engagement and marriage, lessons which helped greatly to keep girls safe from abortion. "These days," one OMW respondent, "some men escort their wives into abortion clinics; they view it as a birth-control measure. It is truly a difficult thing, yet it is truly happening among us, even right within the church. We need to begin teaching about it so that members are properly exposed."

The foregoing FGD reports show that the AIC does not teach about termination of pregnancy in its church meetings. Discussions with various members reveal that they desire to see pastors move beyond exhortations for holiness and Christian service, in order to begin teaching lessons, sermons or seminars on human sexuality, pregnancy and termination of pregnancy. The points emerging from the discussions show that members have made their own individual private efforts to learn about termination of pregnancy.

The Quest for Human Dignity in the Ethics of Pregnancy Termination

Church Action and Discipline on an Unmarried Pregnant Woman

Respondents in all the FGDs reported that the church excommunicates every woman who becomes pregnant outside marriage. As soon as the Local Church Council (LCC) receives reliable information that a certain unmarried woman is pregnant, her excommunication becomes an agenda item at the next scheduled meeting. At such a meeting, the woman's sexual sin is discussed and a decision is reached that she must be excommunicated. This means the congregation is formally and publicly informed that she has been placed under church discipline, as a result of which she will not participate in the Holy Communion services. She cannot sit in the church during communion, she cannot touch the communion elements, and she cannot actively participate in church activities like choir, public Bible reading, preaching, hymns leading, teaching Sunday school, youth activities, and church elections. The church says she is not holy anymore. All other members understand and look at her as a sinner who cannot be a "full worshipper" until the disciplinary period passes. This action also limits her freedom of fellowship with other Christians. If she had been a Sunday school teacher, she has to stop teaching. In MYM a respondent referred to this action as suspension, while MYW simply described the action in the phrase, "She is sent away." Normally, one under suspension would be returned to fellowship about three months after she gives birth.

From MMM reports were made that some church members will start the process of discipline at home. The father of the pregnant girl can send her away from home to go live with her maternal grandmother. In some cases, the pastor will ask her what may have happened, before explaining to her the stand of the church. The church may communicate to her the decision to excommunicate in private, rather than in public. Such decisions are normally recorded as minutes of the Local Church Council. There are cases in which the person simply withdraws herself and goes away with guilt. She may seek and join another denomination where she may find acceptance and care.

In three FGDs (PYM, OMM and MYW) respondents used the terms stigmatization and condemnation to describe what such a pregnant woman experiences in the church. She is stigmatized since she is treated as a worse sinner than the others, including the man responsible for the pregnancy who goes free, undergoing neither investigation nor discipline. Because the magnitude of a woman's sexual sin is viewed to be huge, the shame she experiences is proportionately huge. No church elder or pastor prays for her publicly, and no one spends time teaching her. She becomes only a subject of low-tone discussions, and she experiences social rejection. Her baby, when born, is not dedicated in the church's infant dedication services. If the child grows up and accepts Christ, he or she will be baptized as a member of the church on his or her own account. She is avoided by fellow Christians and is not invited to any events of the church. She experiences further condemnation when her pregnancy is publicly quoted to teach others on moral conduct. This is the same way the church officially deals with any woman who terminates a pregnancy, although this very rarely comes to the attention of church leaders. A respondent in OMM observed that sometimes male church leaders are involved in causing the pregnancy; in such cases no disciplinary action is taken.

The need for counseling in the church was reported in all the FGDs as a way of helping teenagers prevent premarital pregnancy and termination of pregnancy. Respondents noted the obvious lack of counseling within the church, leaving those who find themselves with unwanted pregnancies desperate and exposed. Counseling was also seen to be a possible means of helping the youth in responding to negative peer pressure. It was noted that pregnancy termination also occurred among married women, and they too needed counseling in the church. In both OMM and PYM, respondents observed that many pastors and church elders lacked training in counseling, and were unable to provide professional help to the Christians, making it necessary for the church to plan for in-service counseling courses for its leaders. Three FGDs (MYM, OMM, and PYM) suggested that, in order to reduce termination of pregnancy, the church should show acceptance and love to the pregnant girls.

Treatment of Female Students in Educational Institutions

With regard to the treatment of female students in educational institutions, the FGDs reported a difference between the practice before the 2010 constitutional change and the current practice, as well as a variance in various institutional levels from primary and secondary schools, all the way to colleges and universities. Prior to 2010, pregnancy tests were regularly and periodically carried out in primary and secondary schools to establish the status of individual girls, and any female student found pregnant was expelled. In 2010, a new constitution was promulgated that caused positive changes in educational legislation and regulations governing school life for female students. Pregnancy among school-going girls was seen as a shameful occurrence that needed to be discouraged by all means. After 2010 regulations were amended to allow pregnant schoolgirls to stay in school until close to delivery time when they take leave of absence to deliver, nurse the baby, then go back to school. A respondent in MMM stated that no girl child goes out of school due to pregnancy these days because of the human rights regulations in place. Another respondent in the MYW reported there is a girls' school sponsored by the Anglican Church: they let the pregnant girl stay in school, they take care of her until the advanced pregnancy stage demands that she goes home to deliver, then she takes time at home to care for the baby. Once the baby matures up enough, the girl returns to school. But if she terminates the pregnancy, she is expelled from the school.

In the OMW respondents explained the challenges that are now emerging as a result of the new liberal school regulations. They said that, because female students are now allowed by the government regulations to come back to school after giving birth, this has led to laxity in the moral commitment of the students. A respondent explained a specific case as follows:

> There is a case of one schoolgirl who has given birth to three children. She had one when she completed KCPE, then had another one while in Form II; recently she got pregnant in Form IV and gave birth. Other girls now think this is the norm. These days we (teachers in schools) carry out pregnancy tests in school; once a pregnancy is detected, we call the parents and advise them accordingly on how to care for the girl until she gives birth, after which we advise them to transfer her to another school. We do this to try to work against the laxity in morality among students due to the new regulations. The responsible boy, if in the same school, has to be expelled.

The Ministry of Education places emphasis on counseling, and has ensured that every school has established a functioning Guidance and Counseling Department, where pregnant school girls receive counseling services. Normally they are advised to carry the pregnancy to term, deliver, nurse the baby, then come back to school. This ensures the girl's future is not ruined on the basis of one sexual mistake. At university level, apparently there is a more liberal atmosphere where pregnancy remains the choice of the female student at any time, since sexuality is treated as a private affair and the students are presumed to be more mature. However, in Kenyan Christian universities, pregnancy among single female students is strictly not allowed, and normally results into expulsion. Respondents in MMM observed that schools sponsored by the Catholic Church or the AIC Church teach and instill moral principles that must be observed by all the students. In such schools, female students who become pregnant are excommunicated in the same way it is done in the church. Counseling is done to prevent potential desperation that may sometimes lead to suicide. The MYW respondents pointed out that church-sponsored schools should be in the lead in showing how vulnerable women should be taken care of. They should embrace the pregnant girl, be her refuge, give her a chance, love her, and provide her with counseling. This is needed in cases of pregnancy as well as in termination of pregnancy. They should establish the manner in which the pregnancy occurred, such as rape, incest or other challenging event.

It emerged from respondents in OMM, OMW, PYM, and PYW that there is need for strong counseling departments in church-sponsored institutions to deal with both teenage pregnancy and termination of pregnancy. A student who terminates a pregnancy should be checked medically, treated and returned to school because her future remains important. In OMW a respondent expressed disappointment that modern laws, created because of human rights activism, are the ones encouraging immoral behavior in schools. But a respondent in PYM discouraged the view that schoolgirl pregnancy is a shameful thing because it led to stigmatization in which society does not welcome the girl and her child, leading to termination of pregnancy, which is further condemned by the same society. Even in institutions of higher learning, stigmatization forces a pregnant woman to stay away from classes. In PYM it was noted that subjecting girls to pregnancy tests was a degrading human experience that made Christians think of pregnancy as the worst human mistake one can make. Tension remained strong as other respondents affirmed that schools were educational institutions, and not places for nurturing motherhood or restoring women who had committed abortion.

Prohibition or Legalization of Termination of Pregnancy

All the FGDs agreed that termination of pregnancy must remain illegal, and stated various reasons for this stand. The reasons included the biblical command against killing, the need to keep in place a strong morality check, the need to allow the innocent fetus to live, the psychological trauma resulting from termination of pregnancy, the need to protect the woman's future reproductive capacity, preventing complications resulting from abortion, and the general inclination to protect human life. However, all the FGDs also freely discussed various reasons or circumstances in which termination of pregnancy needs to be permitted. They are as follows: there are usually circumstances when the mother's life is at risk; the need to remove stigma from both pregnancy and its termination; rape of an underage girl who may also be an orphan; the pregnancy may be in the fallopian tube; pregnancy as a result of incest; and severe disability of the fetus.

Decision Making over an Intended Termination of Pregnancy

The most preferred choice for consultation, in cases where a young pregnant girl may be contemplating termination of pregnancy, is the girl's parent. All the FGDs pointed this out, saying that parents are the most understanding people in the event of a pregnancy, whether it is wanted or unwanted. Respondents in MMM recommended that hospital staff should not give any advice to women who have unplanned pregnancies. Someone in the church can talk with her. The best thing is for someone to walk with her as a counselor to encourage her to carry the pregnancy to term, but not help her procure termination of the pregnancy. The person needs counseling, or someone who can persuade. The pastor should come in and help in the pastoral counseling process. From MYM the proposal is that, if she is under-age, she should consult the guardian responsible for her welfare. If she is above the age of eighteen she should make her own decisions. The courts of law should not be consulted because the judge will use the law, without knowing the situation or what the girl is undergoing. The girl should not consult the doctor, or the judge or the man involved; instead she should consult the parents because they feel with her. If the girl does not have any relatives, she should go to the hospital ethics board to evaluate the pros and cons of termination of pregnancy, where they can advise her. The respondents in OMM, OMW, and the MYW ruled out any involvement of the courts of law, and advised that the girl should seek help from the responsible man, her own parents, a medical doctor and a counselor. Both PYM and PYW were skeptical of the involvement of doctors whom they perceive to be only interested in money. All the FGDs viewed parents as the best allies in cases of pregnancy.

Research Findings

Church Action on Pregnancy Termination

The MMM responded that the church may not know of a pregnancy termination, until it is too late. In most cases, it remains a mystery that the church only gets to know if the woman herself admits. As such, action is normally not taken. But as soon as it is confirmed that she terminated a pregnancy, the woman is excommunicated immediately. This is because the church considers pregnancy termination a second sin in addition to the pregnancy out of wedlock. Other FGDs did not provide responses to this question, citing the difficulty of knowing whether any specific suspected abortion was spontaneous or deliberate.

How the Church Ensures Human Dignity

All the groups agreed that confidentiality should be maintained by the church officials handling issues related to unresolved pregnancies. Advice should be given, but not publicly at the pulpit, as is often done by some church ministers. Keeping confidentiality in counseling is an absolute necessity. While some people may use phrases like "she has a ball" to castigate her, adults know how tough it will be for her and can assist her in dignity. The church must avoid all public rebuke of persons who become pregnant or those who terminate pregnancies. MYM respondents advised that an expectant woman should stay out of public limelight until she delivers her baby. She should be embraced and encouraged by the church through private counseling. All the FGDs pointed out that she should be helped to join a support group to avoid stigmatization. The church leadership should form a group for single mothers where they are encouraged through the Bible. Counseling in the church should include group therapy.[1] The church should deal with the issue head-on following the example of Jesus who condemned the sin but forgave the sinners. Therefore the church should condemn abortion but embrace and accept the ladies who get pregnant out of wedlock.

All the FGDs placed high priority in counseling as a ministry that is necessary in all local churches. In the process of doing counseling for any pregnant woman or any woman who terminates a pregnancy, confidentiality is highly emphasized as a requirement. This will help ensure that, in all

---

1. In group therapy people will encourage one another because they will meet other people who are like them; therefore, they will feel they belong.

stages, the dignity of the woman is maintained. The church is advised to avoid all forms of stigmatization and discrimination. Instead the church should be accommodative and work toward restoration. Gossip must be avoided by Christians, as it damages reputation and makes pregnant women seek termination. The responsible boy or man also needs to be identified and counseled. In one FGD a respondent regretted the church's practice of excommunication:

> This excommunication thing is just too shameful. There needs to be a better way. They should just talk to her and ask her to deal with it privately. Like confess her sins to God and then come and take communion. I don't think the Bible teaches that a pregnant unmarried girl should not participate in the communion service. It just says you examine yourself. (PYM)

The perception here is that excommunication is not a biblical practice, and does not encourage the Christian teaching of repentance and forgiveness in cases of pregnancy out of marriage.

Awareness of any pregnancy or abortion in the church

From MMM, when a girl got pregnant before marriage, her family accepted the pregnancy to avoid bringing public shame to the pastor who impregnated her. However, the girl went ahead and terminated the pregnancy. In the same FGD, there was awareness of two pregnancy terminations, about which the church did nothing because it was not officially informed.

From MYM, there was awareness of two young women who became pregnant. The first girl was forced by the parents to marry the man who had made her pregnant. For the second one, the parents were disappointed with the pregnancy but accepted the girl. But they could not accept the man who had made her pregnant because he was from another tribe. The same FGD, as well as MYW, reported that there was a girl who got pregnant and had so many frustrations that she left the church. They also knew of a lady who terminated a pregnancy against the advice of her parents, but did it because of the advice of her boyfriend.

The MYW also reported a case in which the pregnant girl's father chased away both the girl and the mother, not wanting to live with the shame the pregnancy had brought. The remaining FGDs (OMM, OMW, PYM, and PYW) all knew of one case each, in which the church had actually excommunicated a pregnant girl, and had done the same for a girl who had terminated a pregnancy. In the PYW, a respondent reported of a case in which the church pastor had talked publicly about a girl's pregnancy; the family protested and left the church.

General Comments

From the FGDs there emerged a number of general comments that are relevant in the research. Respondents in the MYM advised that the church leadership should openly preach and teach sex education issues in the church so that the youth does not get misleading advice from other sources. They observed that the youth are physically capable of getting children out of wedlock. Therefore, they should not feel they are spiritually strong; instead they should always remember they are vulnerable and at risk. They pointed out to the young men that the best way for the Christian young men to live with girls is to protect the girls around them. Jealously guard her, protect her and do not lead her to a situation that will lead to pregnancy and lower her dignity; so that she can one day be proud of you.

The MYW, PYM, PYW, and OMM also emphasized that the church leadership should teach about chastity, and that discussions between youth and parents need to be encouraged to include sexuality issues. Opinions of the youth need to be heard; such opinions must not be used against them. Parents must be careful in handling pregnant teenage girls so that they do not do abortion. The church should accept repentant sinners without condition. The church needs to set aside specific Sundays and seminar days to teach about sexuality, pregnancy and abortion. Counseling should be preventive, and not wait to deal with problems. Boys who make girls pregnant should also be sought and talked to so that they also confess their sins. Girls don't get pregnant independently, but somehow the church always deals with the girls, and not the boys. The church needs to plan carefully on how to deal with this imbalance.

SUMMARY OF KEY FINDINGS

An analysis of the strengths, weaknesses, opportunities and threats (SWOT analysis) of the AIC church's situation, especially through the FGDs, revealed issues that, if given adequate attention, could help alleviate the ethical challenge of termination of pregnancy.

Strengths

The research revealed the high level of awareness, among church members, of the ethical issues related to termination of pregnancy. There is also awareness of what the church needs to do to help the members, such as counseling, teaching, acceptance, tolerance, and treatment with dignity. Members are aware of occurrences of either pregnancy out of marriage or termination of the same.

Weaknesses

The FGD results indicated that church members never heard any teachings or preaching in the church on the problem of pregnancy termination. This indicates that members received their teachings on this subject from other sources. With regard to how schools treat pregnant schoolgirls, there is inconsistency in implementation of new policies in light of the constitutional rights. While in some schools there is acceptance and tolerance, in others there is suspension and expulsion, revealing lack of a collective approach. There is no systematic teaching of men on how they should relate with women non-sexually within the church context.

Opportunities

There is a general desire among church members to see their pastors engage in discussions on ethical issues that affect their lives. This is a significant opportunity that church leaders needed to take advantage of in order to enhance their members' exposure, interaction and understanding of the ethical subject of termination of pregnancy. The other significant opportunity is the members' call for counseling services within the context of the church.

Threats

The influence from the West, the impact of the media, especially the Internet, and general lack of information from the church, are external threats responsible for the moral decline in society in general and the church in particular. Excommunication, stigmatization and condemnation are the strongest internal threats to morality in the church, since the fear of them leads members to terminate pregnancies out of marriage.

CONCLUSION

The findings from the FGDs reveal various perceptions and attitudes of the Christians in regard to termination of pregnancy. The groups recognize that pregnancy out of marriage is sin, while pointing out that termination of pregnancy is an action women take because of the ways in which the church deals with pregnancy out of marriage. The excommunication, church discipline, suspension from participation in public worship, and deliberate stigmatization all cause loss of human dignity for the pregnant woman. Termination of pregnancy is either a way of attempting to avoid these, or a response to these actions taken by the church. The FGDs further propose various ways of dealing with the problem, focusing especially on counseling at all levels within the church, in addition to regular teaching on issues of human sexuality and termination of pregnancy.

CHAPTER 7

DISCUSSIONS, EVALUATION AND RECOMMENDATIONS

INTRODUCTION

The foregoing data analysis reveals that the church's approach to the theological-ethical challenge of pregnancy termination perpetuates the problem in Kenya, hence the continued quest for human dignity. The literature reviewed and the theories discussed addressed the issues raised by the findings of the FGDs, thereby confirming the direct link between the literature review and the ethical theories on the one hand, and FGD findings on the other hand.

HUMAN DIGNITY

The research, through the FGDs, revealed that human dignity is denied to women who become pregnant outside marriage in a multifaceted way. Some fathers send them away from home, they are publicly condemned in some churches, they face disciplinary procedures in both school and church, and their boyfriends deny responsibility for pregnancy. The socioeconomic pressure leads them to pregnancy termination, which leads to further denial of human dignity by both the church and society. In

Christian ethics, the dignity of the human person is rooted in his or her creation in the image and likeness of God, thereby providing for individual human beings the right to exercise freedom. This should prompt church leaders to develop deliberate action plans and teachings that will inculcate human dignity to those who apparently least deserve it, such as the young women who get pregnant outside marriage and those who terminate their pregnancies. Dignity appropriately bestowed on people will accord freedoms and rights, including the freedom to make mistakes and learn from them. The church must recover its lost ground as the custodian of attributes of human dignity in both theory and practice in order to be truly salt and light in the human world.

STIGMATIZATION

Stigma emerged from the FGDs as a social vice that can be produced and reproduced through a cascade of consecutive social process applied on women. Link and Phelan have outlined components of stigma as follows:

> In the first component, people distinguish and label human differences. In the second dominant cultural beliefs link labeled persons to undesirable characteristics—to negative stereotypes. In the third, labeled persons are placed in distinct categories so as to accomplish some degree of separation of "us" from "them." In the fourth, labeled persons experience status loss and discrimination that lead to unequal outcomes. Finally, stigmatization is entirely contingent on access to social, economic and political power that allows the identification of differences, the construction of stereotypes, the separation of labeled persons into distinct categories and the full execution of disapproval, rejection, exclusion and discrimination.[1]

Stigmatization reaches its worst limits when the categorization, labeling, disapproval, rejection, exclusion, and discrimination are developed and applied by the church upon its faithful members, or by Christians upon their fellow Christians. The manner in which the church treats its members when they fall into the sins of pregnancy and abortion fits a conceptualization of stigma as an attribute that is deeply discrediting; one that negatively changes the identity of an individual to a tainted, discounted one.[2]

---

1. Link and Phelan, "Conceptualizing Stigma," 367.
2. Kumar et al.,"Conceptualizing Abortion Stigma," 1.

According to Kumar et al., abortion stigma is a negative attribute ascribed to women who seek to terminate a pregnancy that marks them, internally or externally, as inferior to ideals of womanhood.[3] A woman who seeks an abortion "is inadvertently challenging widely-held assumptions about the essential nature of women," thereby further challenging the inescapability of maternity and defying reproductive psychology.[4]

The church in Kenya should lead the way in fighting negative stigma among women who have fallen into sins related to sexuality and termination of pregnancy. Stigmatization is, in itself, a serious corporate sin of the church that should be confessed by the leaders and members. Rather than tolerate or even promote stigma, the church should promote love, acceptance, tolerance, and care for those who find themselves in difficult ethical situations in which their choices are severely limited. In this way, the church will fulfill Christ's supreme law of love.

LEGAL FRAMEWORK

Both the Constitution and the Penal Code clearly and unequivocally prohibit termination of pregnancy.[5] This general understanding and interpretation is common among Christians, as expressed in all the FGDs during the research. However, Kenya Christian Church Leaders, while campaigning against the Constitution in 2010, had expressed a different viewpoint. Their understanding of Article 26 (4) was that "if the Draft Constitution 2010 is passed as it is, then doctors, nurses, clinical officers, mortuary attendants and even first aid attendants will be allowed to carry out abortions for all manner of reasons."[6] This was in response to the provisions allowing the opinion of a medical practitioner to determine the validity of a need for pregnancy termination. It is possible that the church leaders indulged in exaggeration in order to drive the point home among Christians. But their understanding differs significantly with that of the Christians who, in the FGDs had explained that pregnancy termination was illegal, and suggested that it remains so, except when life was threatened.

3. Ibid., 2.
4. Ibid.
5. Constitution, 24; and Penal Code, 158–60.
6. Kenya Christian Church Leaders, "Ten Reasons to Vote No," 29 July 2010 (NCCK Communications), 30.

The other legal challenge comes from the fact that legal education focusing on termination of pregnancy is not available to the public in general and the church members in particular. Besides, the lack of prosecution on anyone involved in termination of pregnancy leads to legal apathy among the general populace. Furthermore, the AIC Constitution—the 1952, 1971, 1981, and 2008 (current) editions—has no provisions at all for contemporary theological-ethical issues such as termination of pregnancy. This is an irony close to hypocrisy, given the protest the church put out against the country's draft Constitution (2010), demanding that it must clearly prohibit abortion if the church were to support it at the national referendum.

EXCOMMUNICATION AND CHURCH DISCIPLINE

Reports from the FGDs reveal that the church's favorite disciplinary action taken on members who fall into sexual sin is excommunication, which involves exclusion from participation in the Holy Communion. It is applied through a public announcement to other communicants the reason for the exclusion of a named member due to a specified sin. The manner in which this action is taken bestows public shame on a church member. It also provides opportunity for other members to make scornful and condescending remarks about the sinner. It is supplemented by other measures of church discipline such as stoppage from public worship or corporate church activities. Excommunication is the church's best way of expressing its disapproval of a member's grievous engagement in sin, as well as discouraging others from involving in the same. However, its application is an affront on human dignity, the protection of which is a primary duty of the church.

PASTORAL COUNSELING AND ETHICAL TEACHINGS

The call for organized pastoral counseling in the church emerged from all the FGDs, which also pointed out the lack of it in the local churches. Counseling is needed to regulate sexual attitudes and behavior among youth and adults, to prepare couples for marriage, when an unmarried woman becomes pregnant. It is further needed when a woman is considering termination of pregnancy, as well as when she actually terminates it. When the church fails to avail counseling services to its members, they are left vulnerable and helpless. The call for counseling in the church is a clear indicator of the trust Christians bestow on the church as a reliable source of spiritual, social, and moral principles.

In one FGD it was pointed out that there is a general lack of preparedness among clergy to provide counseling services in the church. This may be due to weaknesses in the curricula for training clergy in Bible and theological colleges, where, as the naming indicates, the emphasis is on Bible and theology. If counseling will remain in the periphery of curricula for training pastors, the church will remain weak in its attempt to initiate and sustain the provision of counseling services focused on matters of morality. Furthermore, the provision of such counseling services will need standardization through counseling manuals for pastors.

The AIC Church has a Christian Education Department through which various groups in the local churches are taught, trained, and helped to grow spiritually. The two most visible and active groups are the Christian Youth and the Women's Fellowship. In these groups, the church teaches an elaborate Bible-based curriculum that addresses specific needs within each group. In the personal experience of the researcher, who is an ordained church minister in the AIC, the lessons taught in these groups are for biblical, doctrinal, and spiritual formation. From the FGDs, it was revealed that the church does not teach on ethical issues in general and termination of pregnancy in particular. Respondents asked that the church considers integrating matters of sexuality and pregnancy, including termination, into its educational programmers.

THE COMPROMISE THEORY

Benjamin suggests the possibility of a legislative compromise which, if applied in Kenya, will acknowledge national ambivalence and divisions rather than papering them over. Concessions need to be made by both sides of the debate that must somehow see the compromise position as splitting the difference between them.

> One possibility is to permit early abortions—during the first trimester perhaps, or more restrictively, some earlier portion thereof, such as the first ten weeks—and to prohibit later abortions except in unusual and extreme circumstances (for example, serious threats to the mother's life or health; pregnancies resulting from rape or incest that are either undetected or psychologically denied

Discussions, Evaluation and Recommendations

by the pregnant women until after the "no questions asked" cut-off point; determination that a fetus is anencephalic . . .)[7]

Benjamin's proposal would enable extreme liberals to retain full freedom of choice during the period within which the majority of abortions are performed, but they would have to agree to a prohibition on second- and third-term abortions except in certain specifically determined circumstances. Extreme conservatives would gain a strong prohibition on second-term abortions (and perhaps late first-term terminations as well) but would have to concede the legal (though not moral) permissibility of abortion during the first term. Benjamin suggests that a law on pregnancy termination that is permissive during the earliest stages of pregnancy but increasingly restrictive somewhere around the beginning of the second trimester may thus be regarded as splitting the difference between the polar positions and providing the basis for a mutually acceptable, integrity-preserving compromise.[8]

The proposal for compromise is further supported by Smedes who argues that society cannot, in all honesty, be absolutist. "We ought not to legislate that every fetus—regardless of age—has unconditional priority over the needs of a mother. We ought not to commit society to judge and sentence every woman who has an abortion as if she were a murderer."[9] Smedes goes on to suggest guidelines for legislation on termination of pregnancy that would protect the rights of the living fetus and be responsive to both "the limits of our knowledge and the concerns of pregnant mothers."[10] Smedes' three-point proposal are that termination of pregnancy should be legally permitted during the first six weeks of pregnancy; should be severely restricted after the first six weeks and through the twelfth week; and should be a crime after the third month.

---

7. Benjamin, *Splitting the Difference*, 166.

8. The proposed compromise would hit a challenge on the matter of termination due to fetal deformity, since amniocentesis, which is the principal method of prenatal diagnosis, cannot be performed until late in the first trimester or early in the second. Terminations for various defects detected by amniocentesis are therefore normally performed in the second trimester and would be prohibited by this compromise. A possible further compromise can be negotiated to permit some, but not all, post-amniocentesis terminations.

9. Smedes, *Mere Morality*, 143.

10. Ibid.

ANALYSIS

In this thesis, the analysis of the problem of termination of pregnancy in Kenya will be based on Martin Benjamin's ethical theory of compromise. In adopting this methodology, a number of factors have been taken into account. First of all, many pregnant women opting for pregnancy termination experience the world as a lonely and threatening place. In the world, they feel alienated and marginalized. As church leaders, Christians, politicians, doctors, and lawyers argue out in defense of their exclusive ethical theories, it is the pregnant women who experience grief, worry, and uncertainty. Second, a number of social-economic realities that are persistent in Kenya, such as poverty, unemployment, gender violence, injustice, and exploitation, conspire to make it extremely difficult for pregnant women other than termination of pregnancy. The social impact of both urbanization and industrialization on Kenyan people is in conflict with traditional values of chastity.

Third, Kenya is currently a recipient of many philosophies and ideas, most of which are directly from the West, and many not be compatible with African culture and Christian convictions. Consequently, human sexuality, conception, pregnancy, freedom and childbearing may all be understood differently in today's Kenya. Fourth, the church has, so far, failed to write any clear statements on the problem of termination of pregnancy, perhaps due to seemingly more pressing issues such as HIV-AIDS and constitutional change. Last, globalization has had its impact on the everyday lives of ordinary Kenyans. For example, economic assistance comes to the poor in the context of such programmers as population control, family planning, individual rights and freedom, reproductive action for women.

Situations that make abortion an option in the lives of a pregnant woman are many. But in this dissertation they are deliberately grouped into three categories, which are named "high," "medium" and "low." The high risk category includes the most serious reasons for an abortion, such as the risk of losing the mother's life, rape and incest. The medium risk category includes severe fetal disability and health risks for the mother. The low risk category is the widest one, and includes all the socioeconomic inconveniences such as shame, education, career type, scarcity of resources for upkeep, a journey, existing family size, contraceptive failure and fetal gender diagnosis. The terms "high," "medium" and "low" are given as indicators of the level of seriousness with which the reasons advanced for abortion

Discussions, Evaluation and Recommendations

should be taken. The task of this section is to evaluate the three categories of factors leading to abortion using the integrated ethic.

In the high risk category, the most serious factor is a pregnancy endangering the life of the mother. A severe heart disease, severe hypertension or an ectopic pregnancy may be the cause of such danger. It seems ethically justifiable, in the context of integration, to carry out an abortion deliberately intended to save the life of a mother.

Pregnancies resulting from rape and incest are herein categorized as "high risk" among the situations that lead to abortion. They constitute the most grievous acts in causing physical, emotional and spiritual harm to the woman. They are also the most violent, humiliating and unwelcome means of conception in human culture. Both acts are clearly condemned in the Bible and in all human cultures. A child conceived out of either rape or incest may be socially rejected by society. For the woman, such a child will be a constant reminder of violence and humiliation. She may be ostracized by society, and sometimes she may be blamed for "enticing" the rapist. Within the very strong Bantu and Nilotic cultures in Kenya, even if such a child was to be put up for adoption, only couples who do not know how the conception took place would adopt. In the context of graded absolutism, the greater good may be to free the woman from such pregnancy through an abortion. In this case, rape and incest are deliberately categorized together with the most severe life-threatening diseases, which would kill a pregnant woman. At a more practical level, female victims of rape and incest should receive emergency treatment in order to prevent any likelihood of pregnancy. The position taken in this thesis is that abortion may be justified when the high-risk situations, such as a threat on the mother's life, incest and rape, occur.

There are two factors, which have been ranked as "medium risk": severe fetal disability and risks on the woman's health. These are ranked "medium risk" because they are considered quite serious, yet the availability of solutions from medical science makes abortion morally wrong and unnecessary, even in an integrated ethical system. Severely handicapped newborns are able to survive and live a reasonable life, upon receiving sufficient, suitable and timely medical treatment. Those who are not able to benefit from medical science can be cared for until they die naturally. The moral choice here is not between the life of the fetus and that of another person; rather it is whether the baby should be killed or be permitted to live its full life. Health problems facing pregnant mothers are, in modern days, generally well within medical control. Unless medical indications are that the mother's life is itself at risk, the growing baby should be born at maturity.

The low risk category of reasons for abortion are mostly socioeconomic in nature, and call for liberating action rather than a free license for abortion. Parents, who are ashamed that their daughter is pregnant out of marriage, may put pressure on her to have an abortion. She may, on her own, seek the same out of shame. Her educational goals may be compromised, or she may lack resources for bringing up the baby, or she may just need to take a trip abroad. Her family may already be too large, and will be severely strained with an additional member. A fetal gender analysis may reveal a baby having a sex the mother may be seeking to avoid for social reasons. Among many Kenyan couples, the boy-child is still preferred. The pregnancy may have been a result of contraceptive failure. All these are grouped in the low risk category because they are not really matters of life and death as such. The arguments advanced in relation to the medium risk factors earlier may apply here as well, in support of permitting the fetus's growth to term.

Categories of Abortion Factors:

CATEGORY	TYPE OF RISK FACTOR	VERDICT
High Risk Factors	• Mother's life in danger • Rape and incest	Yes to abortion
Medium Risk Factors	• Severe fetal disability • Mother's health at risk	No to abortion, but may be permissible if the condition worsens.

Low Risk Factors	• Social-economic inconveniences:
	  • Personal or family shame
	  • Education and career
	  • Scarcity of upkeep resources
	  • Existing family size
	  • Fetal gender diagnosis
	  • Contraceptive failure
		No to abortion

Using an ethic of compromise to evaluate abortion, the conclusion is that only the high risk factors should receive any support for any abortion to take place. It is, therefore, herein recommended that abortion should be legalized for three specific reasons: when the mother's life is in danger, when the pregnancy is a result of rape, and when incest is the cause. Both the medium risk and the low risk factors must be solved, or resolved, through the proposals discussed hereinafter.

THE ROLE OF THE CHURCH

In applying the compromise into the problem of abortion in Kenya, we must start by recognizing that no pregnancy is a woman's singular responsibility. Even if she is completely isolated in this world, at least one other person participated in the act that led to the pregnancy. We must start by asking questions about the father and inseminator. The phenomenon where a man gets a woman pregnant and just walks away is unacceptable in the Christian church. A woman's right to choose must never be allowed to become a man's right to use. As Rudy has argued:

> The church's first priority should attempt to remedy those situations where unwanted pregnancy is addressed only as a woman's private problem. Precisely because we are the Christian church—with an existing network for thinking and teaching about ethical behavior—we have the potential to become a model community, holding men responsible for their part in the reproductive act. . . . Pastors should be taught in seminary that her or his responsibility, as pastor, is to bring the man into the situation.[11]

In a very practical way, if the man responsible is a member of any other Christian church, the man's pastor should be invited to attend a discussion. This approach could significantly change the standard where abortion is chosen simply for the convenience of the male. The church also needs to be assisted to reach the understanding that the baby, whether in a wanted or unwanted pregnancy, belongs not only to the two parents, but also to the church. "Congregations need to understand that people with unwanted pregnancies are making choices about someone who, in a very real sense, belongs to the entire congregation."[12] The unborn are, in a very significant way, part of the church's future congregation, membership and ministry.

The research makes specific recommendations because deliberate and specific acts are necessary for solving human ethical problems such

---

11. Rudy, "Thinking Through the Ethics of Abortion," 245.
12. Ibid., 246.

as abortion. Prof. K. Nurnberger, in discussing the ethics of economic life, points out that Christian ethicists have two specific contributions to make:

> First, they have to work out a new vision based on fundamental faith assumptions and the values, norms and goals which this might imply. This is the normative aspect of Christian ethics. And secondly they have to show how ideological rationalizations and legitimizations of destructive self-interest which obstruct the way towards a more wholesome future, whether individual, collective or institutional, can be overcome through the resources of faith in Christ. This is the soteriological aspect.[13]

Therefore, for the Christian ethicist, the faithfulness to the biblical teaching is only part of the story. Applying the tenets of the Christian faith to the situations and social structures that avail abortion as the only alternative to women in desperate situations is required to complete the story. This puts the church in a significant position of responsibility in applying the proposed ethic of compromise in contributing toward a solution. The proposals for the way forward seek to present a new and realistic vision, while at the same time using the resources of faith to redeem human behavior.

The church's attempts at dealing with the problem of abortion in Kenya should begin with discussions on male sexuality. Men have to be trained to understand the responsibilities that go together with the enjoyment of the sex act. Sex is neither a sport nor a rite of passage. It is not a chance to prove manhood. Instead, it is an act of true and genuine love, in which there are responsibilities, such as taking care of an unborn fetus and an infant in the event of a pregnancy. It is the thesis of this dissertation that the church must start by educating the male members. Men need to come to a better understanding of God's definition of manliness. They need to know male virtues of commitment, sacrifice, provision, protection, and unselfish intimacy. They need to practice these virtues in the family and beyond.

In order to effectively reach out to men in the church, five steps are hereby suggested. First, the church should sponsor a youth programmed series specifically designed for young men. Such a program should deal with biblical teaching on sexual matters. Persons leading the program need to encourage an open discussion concerning the teenagers' temptations, fears, pressures, and sexual development. Second, it is necessary for the church to develop a Bible study and life-application series for adult single and married men, with the goal of encouraging sexual purity in both

---

13. Nurnberger, *Theological Ethics*, 152.

behavior and thought. In following the example of Jesus Christ, the men need to be encouraged to foster virtuous interaction with women, both inside and outside marriage. Third, in order to break the myth that crisis pregnancy and abortion are mainly secular problems, pastoral leaders need to emphasize the responsibility that men bear in both cases. Pastors need to speak out clearly against fornication, adultery, and abortion, and people who want to repent of these sins need compassion from the church. Fourth, the local church can network with the nearest crisis pregnancy center, which can offer some service to the church. Whenever a woman or a couple (married or unmarried) is faced with a crisis pregnancy, they need to be referred to the center. Besides, such a center may do an effective abstinence presentation among the teenagers in the church. The local church can also be involved in the ministry of such a center and give value to its work. Fifth, the local church needs to encourage a male leader to seek training and the materials necessary to lead a post-abortion Bible study and peer-support group. Once the chosen leader is adequately trained and ready, the church can publicize the symptoms of post-abortion syndrome among men and invite men within the community to take part in the Bible study. This will help the church in reaching out to men before and after abortion and strengthen the body of Christ.

The church needs to move into the arena of real personal care for women in situations of unwanted pregnancies. An example is that of Cardinal John O'Connor of New York, whose Archdiocese spent more than US$ 5 million to help 50,000 women in situations of unintended pregnancy in the early 1990s. Aware that more resources are necessary, the cardinal points out that "what the Catholic community does is only one aspect of what government and society should be doing."[14] Similar, if not more explicit, action has been taken by Cardinal Thomas Winning of Glasgow, Scotland. Addressing the Society for the Protection of the Unborn Child on 9th March, 1997, Cardinal Winning launched a unique initiative by formally inviting any woman, of any religion or ethnic background, who is facing a difficult pregnancy, under any circumstances, to contact the Archdiocese of Glasgow for help. He told the women:

> Whatever worries or cares you may have . . . we will help you. If you need pregnancy testing or counseling . . . we will help you. If you want help to cope with raising the baby on your own . . . we will help you. If you want to discuss adoption of your unborn child

14. Whitmore, "Common Ground Not Middle Ground," 10.

> . . . we will help you. If you need financial assistance, or help with equipment for your baby and feel financial pressures will force you to have an abortion . . . we will help you. If you cannot face your family, or if pressure in your local area is making you consider abortion, come to see us, we will help you find somewhere to have your baby surrounded by support and encouragement. We will help you. And finally, if you have had an abortion, if you are torn apart with guilt, if your relationship has split up because of abortion, if you are suffering from post-abortion stress, come to see us, we will help you. . . . I make this pledge, today, as a genuine and practical response from the Archdiocese of Glasgow to this fundamental problem facing society.[15]

Churches taking up responsibilities, such as cited above, recognize the important role of Christians in taking steps to improve human life. Creating viable alternatives enable women considering abortion to know that they will not be ground by their problems, and to get assured of real support. Women who have had abortions need hospitality, compassion and love, not condemnation and ridicule. The church must clearly stand for the message that it is for the wretched and sinners that Christ suffered and died on the cross. Of course, the sin must be frankly acknowledged without compromise. But so must the amazing grace and love of Christ be articulated without compromise.

Charles Villa-Vicencio observes that excessive claims of personal autonomy, whether by men or women, have had disastrous social-economic and ethical consequences in society. He seriously questions the unconditional abortion-on-demand notion, and proposes the practice of communal support:

> The African concept of community teaches that each individual is a person only through other persons. It suggests that no woman should be left alone and unsupported to make decisions about abortion. . . . Perhaps it is too much to ask a violated person, a frightened teenager, or an enraged woman, to consult with others in her hour of anger and despair. Decisions made impulsively, out of fear or ignorance can, at the same time have the most disastrous effects.[16]

Villa-Vicencio argues that the availability of pre and post-abortion counseling needs to be an essential and integral part of any legislation on abortion.

15. Winning, "We Will Help You," 235.
16. Villa-Vicencio and De Gruchy, *Doing Ethics in Context*, 74.

He further reasons that, since abortion is a highly sensitive issue, it should not be dealt with in harsh moral rectitude, but in empathy and compassion. He calls this "the high watermark of New Testament ethics."[17] For Villa-Vicencio, this same ethic compels Christians not to give up on the need to create a world where there is justice for women and children, where there is sexual responsibility and where men share responsibility for the children they father. At the heart of this position is a desire to build a world in which women and men are equal and children are cared for—a world, as others have put it, in which abortion is unthinkable. This type of thinking should encourage legislation that reflects compassion.

RECOMMENDATIONS

The information from the research was used to develop recommendations that need to be applied by stakeholders to help alleviate the ethical challenge of termination of pregnancy. The recommendations will be of value, not only to the church, but also to various segments of the population, especially youth and women, the Ministry of Education, education managers, counselors, community health workers, health service providers, church ministers, students, teachers, parents and guardians, and well as researchers. The following recommendations suffice:

Legislative Compromise: Through the compromise theory of Martin Benjamin, the research proposes that the church should lead in public advocacy for legalizing pregnancy termination within the first six weeks of pregnancy in order to deal with pregnancies arising out of rape and incest. Benjamin's compromise persuades extreme liberals to retain freedom of choice during the period with much uncertainty, and allows extreme conservatives to gain a strong prohibition on pregnancy termination after the first six weeks. This may be a suitable way of splitting the difference between the polar positions while preserving the integrity of those holding variant positions. The protection of the needs of a fetus must be done in the context of the well-being of the mother.

Educational Provisions: It is recommended that the Education Act be revised, with a view to making clear provisions for pregnant girls to continue with education after giving birth and nursing their babies. Likewise,

17. Ibid.

churches must introduce counseling programmers, and strengthen existing ones, in order to prevent unwanted pregnancies. Those who get pregnant need compassion and care from the Christian community. Condemnation only drives some to seek abortion. Through the structured interviews and FGDs, it is clear that pregnancy termination among schoolgirls in Kenya is closely linked to the penalties imposed on girls who become pregnant while attending school or college. Such penalties should be removed through clear and deliberate legislation. Such girls should be allowed by law to proceed with their education, but in the context of programmed counseling. Pregnancy should no longer be treated as an educational crime, but as a normal human condition requiring only a break from studies. Expressions like "suspension" or "expulsion" from school, where these relate to pregnancy, must be removed from the vocabulary of educational administrators.

Health Facilities: In Kenya abortion has significant negative health consequences for women of reproductive age. Since medical facilities that are already over-stretched by common preventable diseases such as malaria, diarrhea and vomiting, measles, pneumonia, and sexually transmitted diseases, it would be unwise to introduce legalized termination of pregnancy into the health system at the moment. Certainly, proper equipment with adequate staff training is necessary to empower the health facilities in handling unsafe abortion. The same should extend to the prevention of unwanted pregnancy through the advocacy of the use of contraceptives.

Emergency Treatment: Safer emergency treatment and counseling are key to the medical approach to the problem of abortion. Since abortion remains illegal in Kenya, as of the time of this research, policy makers in the medical profession need to improve emergency treatment in complicated abortion-related cases, in order to reduce resultant reproductive health complications and death.

Preventive Measures: A number of ways have been suggested for the possible prevention of abortion and unwanted pregnancies. These include improving access to quality family planning services, providing sex education and family life education for all, and providing counseling services to those in reproductive age group (usually 13 to 50 years).[18] It is worth adding that contraceptive devices and methods need to be widely available to those in reproductive age, along with adequate education on their usage. In cases of rape, victims need to report to the nearest medical facility where the possibility of a pregnancy can be promptly averted through preventive medicine, such as an oil douche. It is also crucial that information be provided to both women and men on the risks of unsafe abortion.

Adolescent Education: In seeking to strengthen efforts to prevent unwanted pregnancies, it is important to "provide education to adolescent females and males concerning sexuality and responsible decision-making within the context of adolescent relationships."[19] Such an effort should reach out to adult women and men as well. To prevent unsafe abortions, community-based health education should include the risks of unsafe abortion, any available post-abortion care, and how to identify an unsafe abortion provider. The current training of community-based distributors of family planning resources in Kenya need to include contraceptive failure, unwanted pregnancy, abortion and post-abortion care. Networking and referrals between these people and clinic-based, trained health workers also need to be improved.[20] In addition, doctors, nurses and clinical officers should be trained in post-abortion care. They should be either encouraged or guided to charge affordable fees so that women victims of unsafe abortion can find help.

Adoption: Legal procedures regarding the adoption of unwanted babies should be improved to reduce time wasting and frustration of those who want their children adopted. Males who impregnate girls out of wedlock are required by law to support both the child and the mother. This law needs to be implemented more robustly. An act of parliament on responsible non-marital parenthood needs to be put in place to take care of this.

Legal Framework: Although currently pregnancy termination is both unconstitutional and illegal, it is possible that abortion may get legalized in Kenya within just a few years. In the event that it gets legalized, the law

18. Nyamu, "Safe Motherhood," 6.
19. Rogo et al., "Induced Abortion," 21.
20. Ibid.

should make it mandatory for women to be given information about the nature of the fetus, and of the surgical procedures to be followed whenever they request an abortion. Failure to provide such information would, in my opinion, be a serious infringement of the rights of women.

Any legislation on abortion in Kenya needs to adequately involve views from all healthcare providers, especially nurses. In South Africa, where nurses were not consulted about their opinions regarding the legislation on abortion, they were angry and unhappy. A large number of nurses refused to be involved in any way with the women who had an abortion. Some categorically stated that they chose nursing because they wanted to preserve life and promote patient health. They threatened to leave the profession if forced to nurse an abortion patient.[21] The law in South Africa makes provision for the rights of a nurse, but requires the nurse to make his or her viewpoint known in good time so that substitute staff can be arranged if he or she does not wish to participate in the direct termination of pregnancy (Choice of Pregnancy Act, no. 92 of 1996; Constitution of the Republic of South Africa, no. 108 of 1996). Some of the nurses in South Africa verbalized that they experienced inner conflict because they work in a hospital where "babies are born in one unit and babies are murdered in a unit directly opposite the first one."[22]

One noteworthy point is the apathy on the part of Kenyan law enforcement agencies, such as the police and the judges, concerning the prosecution of illegal abortion agents. We do not get media reports of any court cases involving an illegal abortion practitioner. If abortion remains illegal in the country, then those who carry it out should meet the full force of the law.

Traditional Values: Perhaps society should be educated to recover and use positive traditional values. Values such as men educating their sons, and women doing the same to their daughters, on matters of sexuality would help in providing necessary information to the youth. One of the recommendations of the International Conference on Population and Development in Cairo, Egypt, is "to educate girls to protect themselves from the advances of young men . . . because young girls don't really know how to do that. Also, we must educate boys . . . they must be responsible

---

21. Poggenpoel et al., "One Voice," 4.
22. Ibid., 5.

for their sexual behaviour."²³ One of the worst problems in this generation is the inability of parents to find time alone with their children. Besides, due to urbanization and modern lifestyles, grandparents no longer live in one setting with grandchildren, to whom they can give regular informal education. But a way must be found in which family time is spent in the giving of valuable education to younger ones, with regard to human sexuality, dating, courtship and marriages.

Individual Responsibility: In this dissertation, God is seen as a cosmic gardener, who "tends, protects, nourishes individual morality, and helps it to bloom." Laura Burrell explains:

> Some people, like a hot house orchid or fancy rose, do seem to need religion for their morality to have a purpose or justification. Others are . . . able to withstand almost anything on their own. . . . . The relationship between God and morality is as simple as that—God is a parent, gardener, and so on. He strengthens and cushions individual morality, he gives motivation in the form of outcomes: heaven or hell, and justice and order in a sometimes extremely chaotic world.²⁴

In Christian ethical decision-making, however, autonomy cannot be exercised in isolation from the claims of relation with and responsibility toward other human beings. In the Christian understanding of moral existence, it is alien for an individual to decide his or her own fate in isolation. One of the major problems surrounding abortion is the isolation in which many pregnant women have to make decisions regarding the future of the fetus. Versions of autonomy, which violate God's sovereignty over human life, must also be resisted. Human beings exist together and for one another as well. But ultimately they exist for God and for the sake of a close relationship with God. It is in this light that Wheeler's warning becomes relevant:

> Your body is your own in the sense that you are most intimately and inseparably connected with it, and it is the locus and condition of your experience—but it is not a thing over which you can have property rights. You did not buy it, you cannot replace it, you cannot even add an inch to its stature.²⁵

---

23. Sadik, "Empowering Network," 21.
24. Pojman, *Ethical Theory*, 635.
25. Wheeler, *Stewards of Life*, 46.

Decisions regarding abortion may be autonomous decisions of the pregnant woman. But, in a theological ethical context, they need to be made in recognition that each human being is the responsible and accountable steward of the gift of life. Since stewardship does not entail ownership, care must be taken to seek to know God's will in each case.

AREAS OF FURTHER RESEARCH

The first recommendation for further research focuses on population. Due to the limitations of time, resources and capacity, the sample size and geographical area covered in the research was limited to Kisumu County, with some interviews done in Nairobi and Machakos counties. It is hereby recommended that the study be replicated in other counties in Kenya to reveal the perceptions and attitudes of Christians throughout the country. It is further recommended that the Christians in the other churches, other than the AIC, be involved in a future study.

The second recommendation for further research concerns the research methodology. This research was limited to qualitative methods, namely the FGDs, as the means for collecting information from respondents. A future research needs to apply a quantitative method that will reveal responses in terms of population sizes, health indicators, funding and other variables.

The third area of further research is the relationship between religion or denomination and the prevalence of pregnancy termination. This should be of interest to scholars of theological-ethics and medical ethics keen on linking faith with morality trends.

Fourth, a research involving all doctors in Kenya is necessary to determine the variance of expert medical opinions, perceptions and attitudes toward the problem of termination of pregnancy.

CHAPTER 8

CONCLUSION

THE PROBLEM OF TERMINATION of pregnancy is a multifaceted challenge which places the reproductive health of women at risk and causes death of women of reproductive age in Kenya. Although the law in Kenya clearly prohibits abortion, it goes on in a number of private clinics, in villages, in homes, and many other places. Government hospitals, not only in Kenya, but also all over Africa, record a number of daily admissions of illegally induced abortions. The problem is cause for concern in the church where the response, through excommunication and church discipline, is part of the problem rather than providing a solution.

In a mode of study that incorporated literature review together with structured interviews and focus group discussions, the causes, methods and consequences of abortion were discussed along with both a historical review and a biblical-theological reflection on the problem. In conducting structured interviews, the research revealed the perceptions and attitudes of various cadres of Christians, especially church ministers, doctors, lawyers and administrators. These perceptions and attitudes show the conservative position of Kenyans on the problem of termination of pregnancy, with suggestions on how to help those who find themselves with unplanned pregnancies.

The various procedures applied in procuring abortion all appear to be cruel and violent, in the opinion of this writer. They involve heavy loss of blood, pain for the fetus, and emotional drain for the woman. Since abortion is not a life-enhancing procedure, this writer recommends that, if ever abortion gets legalized in Kenya, the law should require a mandatory explanation, in detail, of the procedures to be applied and their consequences in order that the woman may make an informed choice of whether to go ahead with it or not. The research further revealed that most abortions in Kenya, and in Africa for that matter, are illegally procured through crude methods. Therefore, community-based health care providers need to be adequately educated on the dangers of illegal termination of pregnancy, and ways of providing post-abortion care to patients who have terminated pregnancies. Education must also go to the youth, both boys and girls, on sexual purity, the use of contraceptives, the sanctity of human life as from conception, as well as the physical and psychological issues related to pregnancy termination.

The historical review of the problem of abortion proves useful in providing insights into how earlier generations viewed and handled the problem in their own context. It also serves to point out that humanity's problems, ethical ones included, only change in magnitude and sophistication, but not in essence. Likewise, the biblical review gives insight into the biblical-theological roots of much of today's Christian perception on abortion. It seems that the general perception that abortion is a wrong act has strong historical and biblical bases, which should not be ignored in any discussion of the problem.

Legal restrictions abound in many countries in Africa, and Kenya is included among those whose reproductive health is still governed by laws inherited from the former colonial masters. The law clearly prohibits any form of abortion, except where it is medically prescribed for saving a woman's life. But this legal prohibition seems to only exist in the Constitution and the penal code, but leads to minimal reflection in arrests, prosecutions, and convictions. This portrays the picture that the government is in a dilemma. It does not want to be seen (probably by religious groups) to be relaxing abortion laws on the one hand. The law enforcement arm seems to be deliberately restrained so that abortion services, though illegal and unsafe, are not completely stopped on the other hand. But even if and when it gets legalized there will be certain conditions under which abortion will remain illegal. For example, if a woman is served with abortifacients against her will or without her knowledge. Such terminations will need appropriate legal action taken. However, the researcher takes note of the general observation that declaring an act illegal does not necessarily prevent people from doing it.

The researcher, therefore, suggests that a legislative compromise be worked out in which abortion, up to the sixth week of pregnancy, is legalized for the general public for specific medical reasons, but remains a taboo among religious groups, especially churches. In this way, the church can exercise discipline and pastoral counseling on those who get involved, without infringing on the rights of people who do not follow the Christian faith, even if those rights are perceived to be based on a faulty foundation. This suggestion is based on the general principle that the building of Christ's kingdom is by persuasion, not coercion. Our ministry is not in the legalization of perceived Christian laws, but in persuading non-Christians to find the Christian faith the only reasonable alternative. In countries like South Africa, where abortion is legal, the church's challenge is not in having abortion laws repealed, but in educating her members, and society in general, on what to do to prevent abortions from taking place. The church must give all the information, education, and counseling it can give and, thereafter, leave the individuals to make decisions, whether right or wrong.

The church needs to develop and implement training programmers for children, youth, and adults, both male and female. These training programmers need to address human sexuality from a biblical perspective. The author suggests that reaching out to men is a key factor in addressing the problems of unwanted pregnancy and abortion. The church also needs to institute the ministry of caring for the pregnant and desperate girls. Healthcare facilities also need to be strengthened so that complications that arise from unsafe abortions can be effectively managed. Public education needs to target sociocultural issues, which prevent unmarried girls from going for family planning, as much as the church should teach chastity and abstinence among the unmarried. The church also needs to engage actively in teaching members and counseling those who either get unplanned pregnancies or terminate them.

The research had set out to determine the human dignity issues in the ethical challenge of pregnancy termination; to establish the approach of the Africa Inland Church (AIC) to the ethical problem of pregnancy termination; to develop a viable theological-ethical theory applicable to the problem of pregnancy termination; to determine the relationship between the church's approach to pregnancy termination and theological-ethical theory on the problem; and finally to make recommendations to the church based on the findings of the research. These issues have all been addressed and the objectives of the research have been adequately met.

APPENDIX 1

STRUCTURED INTERVIEWS AND FOCUS GROUP DISCUSSIONS

Respondent's Code:
Respondent's Age:
Gender:
Position in Church:
Years of Service:
Local Church:

1. What does the church teach about termination of pregnancy?
2. What does the church do when an unmarried woman becomes pregnant?
3. Does the church implement disciplinary procedures on an unmarried woman who becomes pregnant? How is this done?
4. How should educational institutions under the church treat girls/women who become pregnant out of wedlock while undergoing training?
5. In your opinion, should termination of pregnancy remain prohibited? Or should it be legalised? Why?
6. Who should decide in cases of disputes over an intended abortion? *Tick one*

Appendix 1

- The pregnant woman alone [ ]
- The pregnant woman and her doctor [ ]
- The hospital's ethics committee [ ]
- The courts of law [ ]
- The pregnant woman and her church pastor [ ]
- The pregnant woman and the man responsible [ ]

7. What does the church do when a pregnant woman terminates the pregnancy?
8. Does the church implement disciplinary procedures on a woman who terminates the pregnancy? How is this done?
9. How should the church treat an unmarried woman who becomes pregnant?
10. How should the church treat a pregnant woman who terminates the pregnancy?
11. How should the church ensure human dignity for an unmarried pregnant woman?
12. How should the church ensure human dignity for a woman who terminates a pregnancy?
13. Do you know of any unmarried woman (or women), in the church, who has become pregnant within the last five years?
    a. What did her family do?
    b. What did the church do?
14. Do you know of any pregnant woman (or women), in the church, who has terminated the pregnancy within the last five years?
    a. What did her family do?
    b. What did the church do?

APPENDIX 2

GLOSSARY

Abdominal traumatism: concept of injury to the abdomen, either blunt or sharp.

Abortifacients: agents or drugs that either indicate or enhance the process of abortion.

ACC: Area Church Council, the fourth-level administrative unit of the Africa Church in charge of an area, the comparative equivalent of a diocese in the Anglican Church of Kenya.

AIC: Africa Inland Church

AIDS: Acquired Immuno-Deficiency Syndrome.

AMECEA: Association of Member Episcopal Churches in Eastern Africa, a Roman Catholic organisation.

Amnesia: a neural disease which erases adult memory.

Amniotic fluid: the clear water-like liquid that surrounds the foetus in the uterus.

Anaesthetic misadventure: death or morbidity arising from anaesthetic drugs/gases or their effects.

Anencephaly: absence of the head in a foetus.

Apoptosis: upward displacement or death of cells in the nervous system, leading to mental retardation in newborns.

Appendix 2

Blastocyst: thin walled cystic structure representing an undifferentiated embryonic cell stage.

Caesarean section: operative abdominal delivery of a foetus.

Cardiac output: amount of blood pumped out by the heart per unit of time.

CCC: Central Church Council, the final level administrative unit of the Africa Church in charge of the entire country of Kenya.

Cell progeny: offspring or descendant cells.

Cervical incompetence: inability of the cervix to keep a gravid uterus from aborting.

Cervical laceration: tears on the cervix (spontaneous or iatrogenic).

Chromosomes: genetic components of a nucleus of a cell.

Collagen development: formation of connective tissue fibres.

Conceptus: formative structure following conception.

Congenital anomalies: abnormalities developing in the body of the foetus during embryogenesis.

Craniotomy: the skull of a foetus in the process of being aborted or being born is crushed in order to deliver a dead foetus.

Cytoplasm: part of a living cell that mediates most cell components within it.

DCC: District Church Council, the second-level administrative unit of the Africa Church in charge of districts, the comparative equivalent of a deanery in the Anglican Church of Kenya.

Deep venus thrombosis: a condition of clots of blood with deep-seated large veins.

Diploid complement: the number of structures that contain genetic material in a human cell; they exist in pairs, 22 pairs, with 2 additional sex determining chromosomes.

Down's syndrome: a congenital condition caused by a genetic abnormality of the 21st chromosome and characterised by some physical malformations and some degree of mental retraction; also called mongolism because the facial figure of the victim resembles that of the Mongolian races.

Ectopic pregnancy: gestation formed and developing outside the normal uterine cavity.

Glossary

Endometrium: the innermost third layer of the uterine wall.

FGD: Focus Group Discussions.

Foetal malformation: abnormality of foetal body structure.

Gametes: two cells male and female whose union is necessary in sexual reproduction.

Genotype: genetic characteristic of an organism.

German measles: a contagious viral disease, also called *rubella*, most common in children between three and twelve years.

Haemorrhaging: excessive and frequent bleeding.

Heavy sedation: high dosing of drugs that cause loss of sensitivity to pain.

Hepatitis: inflammation of the liver parenchymal cells.

Hydrocephaly: an accumulation of cerebrospinal fluid in the brain ventricles, causing seizures, mental retardation, and progressive enlargement of the brain, the skull and the head due to excessive fluid pressure.

Hydrogen peroxide: a form of an antiseptic.

Hyper-pigmentation: excessive formation of skin pigment.

Hypertonic saline solution: salty fluid with a higher osmotic pressure than blood plasma.

Insomnia: lack of sleep.

Intracardiac potassium chloride injection: infusion of potassium chloride into the heart chambers.

Intrauterine injection: infusion of any fluid or drug into the uterine cavity.

Intrauterine devise: a contraceptive coil.

In vitro fertilisation: union of two gametes g in a laboratory tube instead of the normal fertilisation sites such as fallopian/uterine tubes.

LCC: Local Church Council, the first administrative unit of the Africa Church in charge of a local church or congregation, the comparative equivalent of a parish in the Anglican Church of Kenya.

Linear albar: the dark hyper-pigmented skin line on the anterior abdominal wall outside during pregnancy.

Male pronucleus: the nucleus of the spermatozoon after it has penetrated the cytoplasm of an ovum.

Appendix 2

Monozygotic twinning: twins forming from the same zygote as a result of fertilisation of one ovum by one spermatozoon.

Neural tube defect: a congenital defect of the brain and spinal cord as a result of abnormal development of the neural tube during early embryonic life, usually accompanied by defects of the skull or vertebral column.

Ovular residue: the remains left after ovulation; also called follicular remnants.

Pelviperitonitis: inflammation of the pelvic peritoneum.

Perinatal death: mortality of a premature, mature, or post-mature baby as a result of a post-partum or intrapartum or antepartum mortality.

Placenta previa: low-lying placenta.

Plastic cannula: uterine suction curettes made of plastic material.

Prenatal diagnosis: a clinical condition investigated and discovered during the antenatal or prepartum period in pregnancy.

Pronucleus: the nucleus of an ovum or spermatozoon before their fusion in the fertilised ovum.

Prostaglandin infusion: injection of uterotonic drugs or prostaglandin to cause abortion.

RCC: Regional Church Council, the third-level administrative unit of the Africa Church in charge of a region, the comparative equivalent of an archdeaconry in the Anglican Church of Kenya.

Renal failure: kidney failure, inability to produce urine.

Sepsis: infection with micro-organisms, such as bacteria.

Septicaemia: bacteraemia, infestation of blood with bacteria.

Syngamy: a method of reproduction in which two individual gametes unite permanently and their nuclei fuse; sexual reproduction.

Os: an opening, outlet, or mouth.

Tay-Sachs disease: a hereditary metabolic disorder causing progressive mental and neurological deterioration resulting in death in early childhood; also known as "amaurotic familial idiocy."

Thyrotoxicosis: hyperactivity of thyroid function.

Glossary

Trophoblast: extra-embryonic peripheral cells of the blastocyst which become the placenta and the amniotic membranes.

Uterine perforations: holes on the wall of the uterus.

Vaginal douche: a therapeutic kit used by insertion into the vagina.

Vaginal suppositories: peculiar tablets specially made to fit in the vaginal cavity.

Viability: chance of survival outside the natural environment.

WHO: World Health Organisation.

BIBLIOGRAPHY

"Abortion Debate: Catholics Castigate Pro-Abortion Activists." *Sunday Standard*, 5 September 1999.
"Abortion Statistics Shame Kenya." Editorial. *Sunday Standard* (Nairobi), 8 November 1998.
"Abortion Stays Illegal." *Daily Nation* (Nairobi), 14 August 1999.
Adams, Jay E. "What Are/Is Christian Ethics?" *Journal of Biblical Ethics in Medicine* 1 (1987) 20–21.
Africa Inland Church Kenya. Constitution. Kijabe, 1952, 1971, 1981, and 2008.
Alvae, Helen, et al. "Abortion: Whose Values? Whose Rights?" *Tikkun* 12 (1997) 54–59.
ANC Daily News Briefing. 5 July 1996.
Anthony, Susan B. *Revolution Magazine*, 8 July 1961.
Arthur, John, ed. *Morality and Moral Controversies*. 4th ed. Upper Saddle River, NJ: Prentice Hall, 1996.
Asthma, Stephen T. "Abortion and the Embarrassing Saint." *Humanist* 54 (1994) 30–33.
Beauchamp, Tom L., and James F. Childress. *Principles of Biomedical Ethics*. 4th ed. Oxford: Oxford University Press, 1994.
Beckwith, Francis J. "Brave New Bible: A Reply to the Moderate Evangelical Position on Abortion." *Journal of Evangelical Theological Society* 33 (1990) 489–508.
———. "Personal Bodily Rights, Abortion and Unplugging the Violinist." *International Philosophical Quarterly* 32 (1992) 105–18.
Belz, Mindy. "It Takes More Than a Village to Depopulate One." *World Magazine* 14 (1999) 18–21.
———. "Unspeakable Delicacy." *World Magazine*, 20–27 May 1995.
Benatar, Solomon R. "Abortion: Some Practical and Ethical Considerations." *South African Medical Journal* 48 (1994) 469–72.
Benjamin, Martin. *Splitting the Difference: Compromise and Integrity in Ethics and Politics*. Lawrence: University Press of Kansas, 1990.
Bevere, Allan R. "Abortion: Philosophical and Theological Considerations." *Ashland Theological Journal* 28 (1996) 45–59.
Bonevac, Daniel. *Today's Moral Issues: Classic and Contemporary Perspectives*. Mountain View, CA: Mayfield, 1992.
Boss, Judith A. *The Birth Lottery: Prenatal Diagnosis and Selective Abortion*. Chicago: Loyola University Press, 1993.

Bibliography

Brody, Baruch. "Opposition to Abortion: A Human Rights Approach." In *Morality and Moral Controversies*, edited by John Arthur. 4th ed. Upper Saddle River, NJ: Prentice Hall, 1996.

Bromiley, Geoffrey W., ed. *The International Standard Bible Encyclopaedia*. Exeter, UK: Paternoster, 1982.

Bube, Richard H. "Pitfalls in Christian Ethical Consistency." *Perspectives on the Christian Faith* 42 (1990) 162–72.

Calhoun, Byron C. "Am I a Murderer?" *Journal of Biblical Ethics in Medicine* 3 (1989) 46.

Callahan, Joan C. "Ensuring a Stillborn: The Ethics of Foetal Lethal Injection in Late Abortion." *Journal of Clinical Ethics* 6 (1995) 254–63.

Calvin, John. *Commentaries on the Last Four Books of Moses*. Vol. 3. Translated by Charles Bingham. Grand Rapids: Eerdmans, 1970.

Camp, S. Talcott. "Why Have You Been Silent? A Brief Look at the Church and the Abortion Ban in South Africa." *Journal of Theology for Southern Africa* 91 (1995) 59–74.

Carlson, Allan. "The Malthusian Budget Deficit." *Human Life Review* 11 (1985) 35–47.

Catholic Bishops of Ethiopia and Eritrea. "One of the Problems Facing Family Life at the Present Time." *AMECEA Documentation Service*, ADS 9–1001 (1 June 1999) 1–7.

Catholic Bishops of Zambia. "Choose Life: A Pastoral Letter on the Sacred Value of Human Life and the Evil of Promoting Abortion." *AMECEA Documentation Service*, ADS 2/199885 (15 February 1998) 1–6.

Chandran, Emil. *Research Methods: A Quantitative Approach with Illustrations from Christian Ministries*. Nairobi: Daystar University, 2004.

Clarke, Liam. "The Person in Abortion." *Nursing Ethics* 6 (1999) 37–46.

Cohn-Sherbok, Dan. *A Dictionary of Judaism and Christianity*. London: SPCK, 1991.

Condon, Guy. "Fatherhood Aborted: The Hidden Trauma of Men and Abortion, and What the Church Can Do about It." *Christianity Today*, 9 December 1996.

Conee, Earl. "Metaphysics and the Morality of Abortion." *Mind* 108 (1999) 619–46.

Constitution of Kenya. Laws of Kenya. Nairobi: National Council for Law Reporting, 2010.

Cross, F. L., ed. *The Oxford Dictionary of the Christian Church*. London: Oxford University Press, 1974.

Currie, Iain, and De Waal, Johan. "Human Dignity." Chapter 10 of *The Bill of Rights Handbook*. 5th ed. Cape Town: Juta, 2005.

Daniels, Charles B. "Having a Future." *Dialogue: Canadian Philosophical Review* 31 (1992) 661–65.

Davis, John Jefferson. *Abortion and the Christian: What Every Believer Should Know*. Phillipsburg, NJ: Presbyterian & Reformed, 1984.

Davis, Ron Lee, and James D. Denney. *A Time for Compassion: A Call to Cherish and Protect Life*. Old Tappan, NJ: Revell, 1986.

Dixon, Rosalind, and Martha Nussbaum. "Abortion, Dignity and a Capabilities Approach." University of Chicago Public Law Working Paper 345, March 30, 2011.

Doig, Desmond. *Mother Teresa: Her People and Her Work*. London: Collins, 1976.

Dolamo, R. T. H. "A Theological Perspective on Abortion." *Acta Theologica* 18 (1998) 1–15.

Downs, Jo Ann. "Opposing Abortion." *Agenda* 27 (1995) 48–54.

Dunnett, Dolores E. "Evangelicals and Abortion." *Journal of Evangelical Theological Society* 33 (1990) 215–25.

Bibliography

East Africa Centre for Law & Justice. Abortion in Kenya. 413 Designs, 8 November 2011. http://eaclj.org/features/abortion.html.

Ejano, Nondo E. "Tanzania: Unsafe Abortion; The Preventable Pandemic That Consumes Thousands of Women's Lives." European Pro-Choice Network. 28 June 2011. http://europeanprochoicenetwork.wordpress.com/2011/06/28/tanzania-unsafe-abortion-the-preventable-pandemic-that-consumes-thousands-of-women%E2%80%99s-lives.

Elwell, Walter A., ed. *Evangelical Dictionary of Theology*. Grand Rapids: Baker, 1987.

Emuveyan, Edward Ejiro. "Profile of Abortion in Nigeria." *Africa Journal of Fertility, Sexuality and Reproductive Health* 1 (1996) 8–13.

Engelhardt, Hugo Tristram, Jr. *The Foundations of Bioethics*. 2nd ed. Oxford: Oxford University Press, 1996.

English, Jane. "Abortion and the Concept of a Person." In *Social Ethics: Morality and Social Policy*, edited by Thomas A. Mappes and Jane S. Zembaty. 4th ed. New York: McGraw Hill, 1992.

Erickson, Millard J. *Concise Dictionary of Christian Theology*. Grand Rapids: Baker, 1986.

Family Planning Association of Madagascar. "Maternal and Child Health: Family Planning and Abortion in Madagascar." *African Journal of Fertility, Sexuality and Reproductive Health* 1 (1996) 53–55.

Feinberg, Joel. "Abortion." In *Matters of Life and Death: New Introductory Essays in Moral Philosophy*, edited by Tom Regan, 256–93. 2nd ed. New York: Random House, 1986. http://www.ditext.com/feinberg/abortion.html.

Field, D. H. "Abortion." In *New Dictionary of Theology*, edited by Sinclair B. Ferguson and David F. Wright. Leicester, UK: Inter-Varsity, 1994.

Finnis, John. "Abortion and Health Care Ethics II." In *Principles of Health Care Ethics*, edited by Raanan Gillon. New York: Wiley, 1994.

Fisher, Anthony. "What Abortion Is Doing to Britain." *Priest and People* 8 (1994) 414–19.

Fletcher, Joseph. *The Ethics of Genetic Control*. Garden City, NY: Anchor, 1974.

———. *Situation Ethics: The New Morality*. Louisville: Westminster John Knox, 1966.

Ford, Norman. "When Does Human Life Begin?" *Pacifica: Australian Theological Studies* 1 (1988) 298–327.

Fowler, Paul B. *Abortion: Toward an Evangelical Consensus*. Portland: Multnomah, 1987.

Fuller, Russell. "Exodus 21:22–23: The Miscarriage Interpretation and the Personhood of the Foetus." *Journal of Evangelical Theological Society* 37 (1994) 169–84.

Geisler, Norman L. *Christian Ethics: Options and Issues*. Leicester, UK: Apollos, 1990.

———. *Options in Contemporary Christian Ethics*. Grand Rapids: Baker, 1981.

Grassian, Victor. *Moral Reasoning: Ethical Theory and Some Contemporary Moral Problems*. 2nd ed. Englewood Cliffs, NJ: Prentice Hall, 1992.

Green, Melody. *Last Days Newsletter* 7, August–September 1984.

Gustafson, James Walter. *The Quest for Truth: An Introduction to Philosophy*. Needham Heights, MA: Ginn, 1992.

Guttmacher Institute. "Facts on Induced Abortion Worldwide." January 2012. www.guttmacher.org.

———. Reducing Unsafe Abortion in Nigeria. 2008 series. http://www.guttmacher.org/pubs/2008/11/18/IB_UnsafeAbortionNigeria.pdf.

Horn, Carl, III. "Abortion." In Elwell, *Evangelical Dictionary of Theology*.

Huffman, Tom L. "Abortion, Moral Responsibility, and Self Defence." *Public Affairs Quarterly* 7 (1993) 287–302.

Bibliography

Hughes, Philip Edgcumbe. *Christian Ethics in Secular Society*. Grand Rapids: Baker, 1983.
Hunt, Geoffrey. "Abortion: Why Bioethics Can Have No Answer: A Personal Perspective." *Nursing Ethics* 6 (1999) 47–57.
Hurry, Stephanie. "Termination of Pregnancy: A Nurse's Right to Choose." *British Journal of Theatre Nursing* 7 (1997) 18–22.
Inch, Morris A. "Ethics." In Elwell, *Evangelical Dictionary of Theology*.
Interlink Rural Information Service. "Kenya's Stand on Abortion Criticised." Horizon. *Daily Nation*, 5 August 1999.
Jakuja, Welekazi P. "An Investigation of the Ethical Implications That Arise for Christians from Contraception and Abortion." BA honours thesis, University of Transkei, 1990.
Johnston, Robert. "Historical Abortion Statistics, South Africa." Last updated 11 March 2012. http://www.johnstonsarchive.net/policy/abortion/ab-southafrica.html.
Jones, Chris. "Euthanasia—How Much Longer?" Manuscript. Faculty of Theology, University of Stellenbosch, November 2011.
Jonsen, Albert, and Stephen Toulmin. *The Abuse of Casuistry*. Berkeley: University of California Press, 1988.
Kahara, Dave. "Facts Abortionists Ought to Consider." Horizon. *Daily Nation*, 16 September 1999.
Kasomo, Daniel. *Research Methods in Humanities and Education*. Egerton: Egerton University Press, 2006.
Kiai, Wambui. "Act Now on Teen Pregnancies." *Gender Review* (1994) 5–8.
Kittel, Gerhard, ed. *Theological Dictionary of the New Testament*. Volume 2. Grand Rapids: Eerdmans, 1964.
Kombo, Donald Kisilu, and Delno L. A. Tromp. *Proposal and Thesis Writing: An Introduction*. Nairobi: Paulines, 2006.
Koop, C. Everett. *The Right to Live, the Right to Die*. Wheaton, IL: Tyndale, 1976.
Kumar, Anuradha, et al. "Conceptualising Abortion Stigma." *Culture, Health & Sexuality*, February 2009, 1–15.
Lammers, S., and A. Verhey, eds. *On Moral Medicine*. Grand Rapids: Eerdmans, 1981.
Lebech, Mette. "What Is Human Dignity?" Faculty of Philosophy at the National University of Ireland, 2012.
Lehman, Paul L. *Ethics in a Christian Context*. Eugene, OR: Wipf & Stock, 1998.
Lema, V. M., et al. "Induced Abortion in Kenya: Its Determinants and Associated Factors." *East African Medical Journal* 73 (1996) 164–68.
Liefeld, David R. "A Pastoral Approach to the Politics of Abortion." *Concordia Journal* 17 (1991) 246–68.
Link, B., and J. C. Phelan. "Conceptualizing Stigma." *Annual Review of Sociology* 27 (2001) 363–85.
Marquis, Don. "Why Abortion Is Immoral." In *Taking Sides: Clashing Views on Controversial Moral Issues*, edited by Stephen Satris. 3rd ed. Guilford, CT: Dushkin, 1992.
Mbiti, John S. *African Religions and Philosophy*. Nairobi: East African Educational, 1995.
McCormick, Richard A., and Paul Ramsey, eds. *Doing Evil to Achieve Good: Moral Choice in Conflict Situations*. Chicago: Loyola University Press, 1978.
McQuilkin, Robertson. *An Introduction to Biblical Ethics*. Wheaton, IL: Tyndale, 1989.
Michels, Nancy. *Helping Women Recover from Abortion*. Minneapolis: Bethany House, 1988.

Bibliography

Moody, Howard. "Abortion: Woman's Right and Legal Problem." *Theology Today* 28 (1971) 338–39.
Moore, Keith. "Abortion: Logical and Theological Considerations." *Bibliotheca Sacra* 148 (1991) 112–17.
Mori, Maurizio. "Abortion and Health Care Ethics I." In *Principles of Health Care Ethics*, edited by Raanan Gillon. New York: Wiley, 1994.
Mugenda, Olive M., and Abel G. Mugenda. *Research Methods: Qualitative and Quantitative Approaches*. Nairobi: Africa Centre for Technology Studies, 2003.
Mumo, Jasper. "The Human Genome Decoded." Special Report. *Sunday Nation*, 2 July 2000.
The New Encyclopaedia Britannica, Micropaedia. Vol. 1. Chicago: Encyclopaedia Britannica, 1990.
Noonan, John T., Jr. "An Almost Absolute Value in History." In *Taking Sides: Clashing Views on Controversial Moral Issues*, edited by Stephen Satris. 2nd ed. Guilford, CT: Dushkin, 1990.
Nurnberger, K. *Theological Ethics: Ethics of Economic Life*. Pretoria: University of South Africa, 1990.
Nyamu, John. "Safe Motherhood: Every Woman's Right." Femalestyle. *Sunday Nation*, 5 September 1999.
Okaalet, Peter, and Jean Kagia. "Abortion: A Medical Christian Perspective." Horizon. *Daily Nation*, 28 October 1999.
Okullu, John Henry. *Church and Marriage in East Africa*. Nairobi: Uzima, 1990.
Olen, Jeffrey, and Vincent Barry. *Applying Ethics*. 4th ed. Belmont, CA: Wadsworth, 1992.
Onyango, Sara, et al. "Scaling Up Access to High-Quality Postabortion Care in Kenya: A Facility-Based Assessment of Public and Private—Sector Facilities in Western and Nyanza Provinces." IPAS. Chapel Hill, NC, 2003.
Osur, J. "Abortion Illegal Only for the Poor." Horizon. *Daily Nation*, 3 August 2000.
Passé, Andre Jules. "State of Unsafe Abortion in Burkina Faso." *African Journal of Fertility, Sexuality and Reproductive Health* 1 (1996) 66–67.
Payne, Franklin E. *Biblical Healing for Modern Medicine*. Augusta, GA: Covenant, 1993.
Pearsall, Judy, and Bill Trumble, eds. *The Oxford English Reference Dictionary*. 2nd ed. Oxford: Oxford University Press, 1996.
The Penal Code. Laws of Kenya, 1973:158–160.
Poggenpoel, M., et al. "One Voice Regarding the Legislation of Abortion: Nurses Who Experience Discomfort." *Curations: South Africa Journal of Nursing* 21 (1998) 2–7.
Pojman, Louis P. *Ethical Theory: Classical and Contemporary Readings*. Belmont, CA: Wadsworth, 1998.
Pope John Paul II. *Evangelium Vitae* [The Gospel of Life]. 25 March 1995.
———. Post-Synodal Apostolic Exhortation. Yaounde, 14 September 1995.
Ramalefo, Cally, and Innocent M. Modisaotsile. "The State of Unsafe Abortion in Botswana: Evidence from Proxy Indicators." *Africa Journal of Fertility, Sexuality and Reproductive Health* 1 (1996) 38.
Rogo, Khama O. "Induced Abortion in Sub-Saharan Africa." *Africa Journal of Fertility, Sexuality and Reproductive Health* 1 (1996) 14–25.
Rudy, Kathy. "Thinking Through the Ethics of Abortion." *Theology Today* 51 (1994) 235–48.
Sadik, Nasif. "An Empowering Network." *Gender Review* (July–Sept 1995) 20–22.

Bibliography

"Safe Motherhood: Every Woman's Right." Lifestyle. *Sunday Nation* (Nairobi), 5 September 1999.

Sai, Fred. "An Overview of Unsafe Abortion in Africa." *Africa Journal of Fertility, Sexuality and Reproductive Health* 1 (1996) 2–3.

Sappington, R. Jay. "Abortion: A Non-controversial Approach." *Trinity Journal* 14 (1993) 183–99.

Schaeffer, Edith. *Lifelines: The Ten Commandments for Today*. Westchester, IL: Crossway, 1982.

Schoening, Richard. "Abortion, Christianity, and Consistency." *Philosophy in the Contemporary World* 5 (1998) 32–37.

Singh, Susheela, et al. "The Incidence of Induced Abortion in Uganda." *International Family Planning Perspectives* 31 (2005) 183–91.

Sjostrand, M., et al. "Socio-Economic Client Characteristics and Consequences of Abortion in Nairobi." *East African Medical Journal* 75 (1995) 325–32.

Smedes, Lewis B. *Mere Morality: What God Expects from Ordinary People*. Grand Rapids: Eerdmans, 1983. Reprint, 2002.

Sprinkle, Joe M. "The Interpretation of Exodus 21:22–25 *(Lex Talionis)* and Abortion." *Westminster Theological Journal* 52 (1993) 233–53.

Steffen, Lloyd. *Life Choice: The Theory of Just Abortion*. Cleveland: Pilgrim, 1994.

Stott, John. *Issues Facing Christians Today*. London: Marshall Morgan & Scott, 1984.

Sutherland, Gail Hinich. "Abortion and Woman's Nature: The Idiom of Choice." *Soundings* 76 (1993) 603–29.

Sutton, Agneta. "Arguments for Abortion of Abnormal Foetuses and the Moral Status of the Developing Embryo." *Ethics and Medicine* 6 (1990) 5–10.

Swindoll, Charles R. *Sanctity of Life: The Inescapable Issue*. Dallas: Word, 1990.

Thiroux, Jacques P. *Ethics: Theory and Practice*. 5th ed. Englewood Cliffs, NJ: Prentice Hall, 1995.

Tienou, Tite. *The Theological Task of the Church in Africa*. Achimota, Ghana: Africa Christian, 1990.

Turkson, Richard B. "Overview of the Legal Situation Regarding Abortion in Sub-Saharan Africa." *African Journal of Fertility, Sexuality and Reproductive Health* 1 (1996) 5–7.

UNESCO Declaration on the Human Genome and Human Rights. 1998.

Van der Spuy, Mervin. "Post-Abortion Syndrome: A Christian Counselling Perspective." *South African Baptist Journal of Theology* 7 (1998) 141–59.

Villa-Vicencio, Charles, and John De Gruchy. *Doing Ethics in Context: South African Perspectives*. Cape Town: David Philip, 1994.

Warren, Mary Anne. "On the Moral and Legal Status of Abortion." In *Morality and Moral Controversies*, edited by John Arthur. Upper Saddle River, NJ: Prentice Hall, 1996.

Weil, William B., Jr., and Martin Benjamin, eds. *Ethical Issues at the Outset of Life*. Boston: Blackwell Scientific, 1987.

Wheeler, Sondra Ely. *Stewards of Life: Bioethics and Pastoral Care*. Nashville: Abingdon, 1996.

White, Andrew. "Abortion and the Ancient Practice of Child Sacrifice." *Journal of Biblical Ethics in Medicine* 1 (1987) 34–42.

White, R. E. O. "Biblical Ethics" and "Christian Ethical Systems." In Elwell, *Evangelical Dictionary of Theology*.

Whitmore, Todd David. "Common Ground Not Middle Ground: Crossing the Pro-Life, Pro-Choice Divide." *Christian Century* 113 (1996) 10–12.

Bibliography

Winning, Thomas Joseph. "We Will Help You: In Praise of Bernard Nathanson." *Catholic International* 8 (1997) 234–36.
Zimmerman, Martha. *Should I Keep My Baby?* Minneapolis: Bethany House, 1983.

INDEX

abortion. *See also* pregnancy termination
  advantages of, 98–99
  arguments against, 45–52
  arguments for, 37–45
  categories of, 116–18
  complications, 9
  consequences of, 62–68
  defined, 14–17
  disadvantages of, 99
  options to, 122
  rates of, 2, 5–8, 63–64
  stigma of. *See* stigmatization
  types of, 15
abortion study. *See* pregnancy termination study
absolutism, 73–76
Adams, Jay E., 18
adoption, 125
Africa, abortion rates, 5–6
Africa Inland Church, 85–86
aloe seeds, 59–60
American Psychiatric Association, 65
anecephalus, 58
Anthony, Susan B., 50
anti-abortionist, 46–47, 71
Aquinas, Thomas, 25
Aristotle, 24–25
Athenagoras, 24
Augustine, 25
avoidance phenomenon, 66–67

backstreet abortion, negative effects of, 8
Beckwith, Francis J., 32
Benatar, Solomon R., 41–42
Benjamin, Martin, 77, 78, 114–15, 123
Bevere, Allan R., 33
biblical perspectives on abortion, 33–34, 130
Binet scale of Intelligence Quotient (IQ), 37
biomedical ethics, 18
Bourne, Rex v., 4n6
British Abortion Law Reform Association, 27
Brody, Baruch, 47–48
Bromiley, Geoffrey W., 71
Burkina Faso, 59
Burrell, Laura, 127
Burundi, 4

Caesarius of Arles, 24
Calhoun, Byron C., 15–16
Calvin, John, 27, 35
Camp, S. Talcott, 58
cannibalism, 23–24
Carlson, Allan, 65
Cartesian dualism, 26
Chandran, Emil, 83
chastity, values of, 56
chemical methods to induce abortion, 59
"child," defined, 96
child abuse syndrome, 43

Index

Children and Young Persons Act, 96
Christian Education Department, 114
Christian ethical theory, 72–73
Christian ethics, 19, 50, 70–73, 76–79, 111, 120–21
church discipline, 2, 113
church leaders
  awareness of pregnancy/abortion, 106–7
  preach sex education, 107
  structured interviews from, 90–92
church teachings on termination of pregnancy, 97–100
church/church action
  Bible-based curriculum, 114
  Christian Education Department, 114
  clergy preparedness, 114
  personal care for women, 121–22
  on pregnancy termination, 105
  role of, 119–123
  training programmers, 131
  on unmarried pregnant women, 100–101
church-sponsored schools, 103
Clement of Alexandria, 24
communal support, 122–23
compensation, 67
compromise theory, 76–79, 114–15, 123
conception. *See also* unborn
  compromise theory, 78–79
  ensoulment and, 25–27
  Genesis narrative, 29–31
  God's relationship before, 32
  preformation theory, 26
condemnation, 100–101
Conee, Earl, 39
confidentiality in counseling, 105
conflicting absolutism, 74, 75
consequences of abortion, 62–68
consequentialist justification, 39–40
Constitution and penal code of Kenya, 3–4, 20, 112–13, 130
contextual absolutism, 74–76
contraceptives, 10, 54–55, 56, 59–60, 124, 130
Corrigan, Billie, 67–68

counseling
  in the church, 113–14
  confidentiality, 105
  need for, 101
  pre- and post-abortion, 122–23
criminal abortion, 14
crisis pregnancy, 121

data collection
  ethical considerations, 87
  procedure, 86–87, 89–90
defense mechanisms to abortion, 67
"A Defense of Abortion" (Thomson), 38–39
Descartes, 26
descriptive design, 84
Deuteronomy, 30
The Didache, 23
dilation and curettage (D&C), 45–46, 60, 62–63
disability diagnosis, 48–49, 57
divine curse, 33
doctors. *See* physicians
Dolamo, R. T. H., 29
double effect principle, 45–46
Downs, Jo Ann, 50, 64
Down's syndrome, 57. *See also* disability diagnosis

early Christian views, 24–26
East Africa Centre for Law and Justice, 8–9
economic effects of abortions, 64–65
ectopic pregnancies, 63
education, 130
education policy, 56–57, 123–24
educational institutions
  Bible-based curriculum, 114
  church-sponsored schools, 103
  counseling departments, 103
  expulsion from, 97
  pregnant girls out of wedlock and, 95
  treatment of female students in, 101–3
Ejano, Nondo E., 6
Engelhardt, Hugo Trustram, Jr., 39–40
English, Jane, 40–41
ensoulment, 25–27

Index

Erickson, Millard J., 15, 46
eternal salvation, 43–44
ethical absolutism, 73–76
ethical hierarchicalism, 74–76
ethics
   biomedical, 18
   concept of, 17–18
   defined, 17
   doctrine and, 71–72
   philosophical, 18
   theological, 18–19
   theology and, 71–72
Ethiopia, 6, 7
Eucharist, concept of, 23–24
euthanasia, 78
Evangelium Vitae, 28
excommunication, 100, 103, 106, 113
Exodus, 30, 33–34, 98
extreme liberal, 78

family planning, 55
Family Planning Association of Madagascar, 62
feminists view, 50
feminists view of abortion, 50
fetal gender analysis, 118
fetus
   compromise theory, 78–79
   disability diagnosis, 48–49, 57
   in image of God, 31
   right to life, 41–42, 50
   right to self-defense, 49–50
   in utero, 31–32
   value before God, 90–91
   woman's right to refuse use of body to dependent, 38
Field, D. H., 15, 72
Fisher, Anthony, 63
Fletcher, Joseph, 37, 75–76
focused group discussions
   church action and discipline on unmarried pregnant women, 100–101
   church action on pregnancy termination, 105
   church awareness of pregnancy/abortion, 106–7
   church teachings on termination of pregnancy, 97–100
   decision making over intended pregnancy termination, 104
   described, 86–87
   group descriptions, 97
   legalization of pregnancy termination, 103–4
   prohibition of pregnancy termination, 103–4
   treatment of female students in educational institutions, 101–3
Fowler, Paul B., 31, 34–35, 48–49
Fuller, Russell, 35

Geisler, Norman L., 73, 74–75
Genesis narrative, 29–31
global perspective, 4–5
globalization, 4–5, 116
God, view of, 76
"good," defined, 73
graded absolutism, 74–76, 117
Grassian, Victor, 39, 61
Great Britain, 63–64
Groote Schuur Hospital, 6–7
Guidance and Counseling Department, 102, 103
Guttmacher Institute, 5, 7

health facilities, 124
herbs inducing abortions, 59–60
Hern, Warren M., 67–68
high risk abortions, 116, 117
high risk category, 116, 117
Hippocrates, 23
historical perspective, 22–28, 130
Hittite laws, 35
Horn, Carl, III, 15
Hosea, 32–33
Huffman, Tom L, 49–50
human dignity, 19–21, 105–6, 110–11, 131
human post-mortem existence in eternity, 43–44
Humanae Vitae, 28
Hurry, Stephanie, 23
hydrocephalus, 58

Index

hysterectomy, 61
hysterectomy abortion, 61

in vitro fertilization, 44–45
Inch, Morris A., 18
indirect abortion, 45
individual responsibility, 127
inducing abortion, 9–10, 58–60
Infant Life Preservation Act, 27
infanticide, 23–24, 61
International Conference on Population and Development, 126–27
Isaiah, 31

Jakuja, Welekeza P., 43
Jeremiah, 31
Jerome, 25
Jesus Christ, 76
John Paul II, Pope, 28
Johnston, Robert, 6
Jones, Chris, 78
justice, to oppose abortion, 48

Kahara, Dave, 63, 65, 66
Kant, Immanuel, 74
Kantian view, 39
Kasomo, Daniel, 83
Kenya, 8–10, 55–57
Kenyatta National Hospital, 9
Kleicharchos, 23
Kombo, Donald Kisilu, 83, 87
Koop, C. Everett, 51
Kumar, Anuradha, 112

late-term abortions, 16
Lebech, Mette, 19–20, 19n50
legal education on pregnancy termination, 113
legal framework, 125–26
legal restrictions, 130
legalizing abortions, 3, 27, 94, 96, 103–4, 114–15
legislation guidelines, 115, 131
legislative guidelines, 115
Lesch-Nyhan syndrome, 58
Link, B., 111
low risk abortions, 116, 118
low risk category, 116, 118

the Luo, 54
Luther, Martin, 27

Madagascar, 59
male sexuality, church's attempt to deal with, 120–21
Malthus, Thomas, 65
Marquis, Don, 46–47
maternal deaths, 6, 7–8
maternal deaths related to abortions, 6
McCorvey, Norma, 28n34
McQuilkin, Robertson, 49
medical dangers in abortion, 62–63
medical factors to pregnancy termination, 57–58
medical problems during/after abortion, 94
medical reasons for abortions, 93
medium risk abortions, 116, 117–18
medium risk category, 116, 117–18
Meme, Julius, 2–3
Michels, Nancy, 54, 65, 66, 67
Ministry of Education, 102
Modisaotsile, Innocent M., 16
mongolism, 57. *See also* disability diagnosis
Moody, Howard, 42–43
moral compromise, 76–79
moral rights, 41
morality, 24, 73, 108–9, 127
mother's rights, 38–39

neural tube defect, 58
Nigeria, 7
Nurnberger, K., 120
nurses
  emotional stress of, 68
  inner conflict of, 126
Nyamu, John, 15

O'Connor, John, 121
Okullu, John Henry, 68
Onyango, Sara, 9

parents, role of, 44, 56, 99, 104, 107, 118
Passé, Andre Jules, 62

Index

pastoral counseling, 113–14. *See also* counseling
Paul, Alice, 64
Paul VI, Pope, 28
Payne, Franklin E., 4, 64
Penal Code. *See* Constitution and penal code of Kenya
personal autonomy, 52
personhood
  concept of, 40
  conditions of, 40–41
  function-based definition of, 51
Phelan, J. C., 111
philosophical ethics, 18
physicians
  psychological well-being of, 67–68
  structured interviews from, 92–95, 97
Pius IX, Pope, 26
placenta previa, 63
Pojman, Louis P., 17, 70
population control through abortion, 23
post-abortion care, 130
post-abortion counseling, 122–23
post-abortion syndrome (PAS), 65–67
post-traumatic stress disorder (PTSD), 65, 66
poverty, 55–56
pre-abortion counseling, 122–23
preformation theory, 26
pregnancy. *See also* pregnancy termination; pregnancy termination study
  among school girls, 101–3
  causal relationship between sexual pleasure and, 49
  church action and discipline on unmarried women, 100–101
  church awareness of, 106–7
  criminalizing, 97
  crisis, 121
  medical implications of, 93
  out of wedlock, 91
  reasonable precaution to avoid, 38–39
  stage of, for abortion, 51
  through rape, 47–48

pregnancy termination. *See also* abortion; pregnancy termination study
  church teachings on, 97–100
  compromise theory, 76–79, 114–15
  as criminal offence, 95
  crude methods used in, 58–60
  graded absolutism, 76
  legalization of, 3, 27, 94, 96, 103–4, 114–15
  medical factors to, 57–58
  medical procedures in, 60–62
  poverty and, 55–56
  prohibition of, 103–4
  social stigma of, 54–55
  socioeconomic factors, 53–57
pregnancy termination study
  analysis of, 116–19
  assumptions, 12–13
  background, 2–5
  conceptual framework, 79–81
  data collection procedure, 86–87, 89–90
  focus groups. *See* focused group discussions
  interviews. *See* structured interviews
  key findings, 107–9
  methodology, 13–14
  population sample/size, 85–86
  purpose of, 11, 89
  rationale for, 12
  research instruments, 85
  research limitations, 13
  research objectives, 11
  research procedure, 84–85
  research questions, 11–12
premature birth view, 35–36
preventive measures, 124–25
primary data, 86–87
pro-choice advocate, 71
pro-choice argument, 46–47, 52
pro-life ethicists, 46–47
prostaglandin infusions, 61
Psalms, 30–31
psychological effects of abortion, 65–68

qualified absolutism, 74–76
qualitative research, defined, 83
quasi-person, concept of, 42

Index

Ramalefo, Cally, 16
rape, pregnancy from
  act of, 27, 47–48, 50
  church teachings, 98–99
  compromise theory, 114
  feminists view of, 50
  legislative compromise, 123
  preventive measures, 117, 125
  support for abortion of, 42–44
rationalization for abortion, 67
repression, 67
research, defined, 82–83
research design, 83–84
research method, 83
Rex v. Bourne, 4n6
right to life, 71, 78
Roe v. Wade, 4, 27–28
Rogo, Khama O., 7, 15, 58, 59
Roman Catholic Church, 26–29, 45–46
Rudy, Kathy, 119

safe abortion, 16, 42
Sai, Fred, 6, 59, 62
saline, 61
saline abortion, 61
Sappington, R. Jay, 54, 65, 66
Schaeffer, Edith, 50–51
Schoening, Richard, 43–45
schoolgirls
  sexual immorality of, 91
  sexual purity, 55, 99
secondary data, 86
secular vocations, 77
severe fetal disability, 117–18
sexual permissiveness among teenagers, 55
sexual promiscuity, 5–6, 91, 96, 100
sexual purity, 55, 99
situation ethics, 37–38
situationism, 75–76
Sixtus V, Pope, 26
Smedes, Lewis B., 115
social consequences of abortion, 64
socioeconomic factors to pregnancy termination, 53–57, 118
South Africa, 4
South Africa, abortion rates, 5–6
Soviet Union, 27

spina bifida, 57. *See also* disability diagnosis
Sprinkle, Joe M., 34–35
stigmatization, 2, 100–101, 105, 111–12
Stott, John, 55, 64
structured interviews
  from church ministers, 90–92
  described, 90
  from doctors, 92–95
  from lawyers, 95–96
suction abortion, 60–61
"sugar daddies," 55
Sumerian laws, 35
suppression, 67
Sutherland, Gail Hinich, 49

Tanzania, 6
Tay-Sachs disease, 58
Teachings of the Twelve Apostles, 23
teenage boys, 56
termination of pregnancy. *See* abortion; pregnancy termination; pregnancy termination study
Tertullian, 23–24
theological ethics, 18–19
theological-ethical perspectives on abortions, 36–45
theology and ethics, 71–72
Thielicke, Helmut, 74
Thiroux, Jacques P., 63
Thomson, Judith Jarvis, 38–39
Tienou, Tité, 72
Tooley, Michael, 42
traditional values, 126–27
traducianism, 46
Tromp, Delno L. A., 83, 87

Uganda, 6
unborn. *See also* conception
  biblical perspectives on, 29–36
  miscarriages and murders of, 32–35
United Kingdom, 27
United Nations, 20–21
United States, 4, 27–28, 63–64
universal moral obligation, 74
unmarried women, 100–101
unqualified absolutism, 73–74, 75

Index

unsafe abortions, defined, 16

vacuum aspiration, 60–61
Van der Spuy, Mervin, 65, 66–67
Villa-Vicencio, Charles, 122–23
violent nature of abortions, 48

Wade, Roe v., 4, 27–28
Warren, Mary Anne, 41
Wheeler, Sondra Ely, 127

White, R. E. O., 72
Winning, Thomas, 121–22
women's right to abortion, 90, 98
women's rights movement, 90
worldly chores, 77

Zambia, 4
Zimbabwe, 6
Zimmerman, Martha, 54